THE

TEMPLE

IN

YOU

When The Holy Spirit Dwells in a man

by

Alice Kalu

All scriptural references and verses included in this book are

sourced from the Holy Bible .

DEDICATION

This book is dedicated to God Almighty, who has translated me from the kingdom of darkness into His marvellous light, has ransomed me through the blood of His Son, Jesus Christ, and has made me a vessel of honour unto His higher calling. For the first time, I had hope.

ACKNOWLEDGEMENT

First and foremost, I want to thank God Almighty for His grace in this milestone achievement and the Holy Spirit for His divine knowledge, wisdom, and teaching in putting up this book. I also wish to thank my parents, my husband, and my children for their love, care, and patience as I worked through this period. Thanks to everyone who has supported me in one way or another, whether through their prayers or by publicising this message.

God bless you all.

ABOUT THE AUTHOR

Mrs Alice Kalu is an anointed woman of God, an evangelist, and a preacher of the Word of God who propagates the gospel by every means at her disposal. She is also a gospel artist who has released anointed songs available on all music platforms on the internet. She is happily married with children, and her life and that of her family are a living testimony to the wonderful power of God.

Table of Contents

The spirit of God in a man is the temple in a man not built by hands. As no man can declare 'Jesus Is Lord' except by the Holy Spirit that dwells in a man.

Do you not know that your bodies are members of Christ himself? Shall I then take the members of Christ and unite them with a prostitute? Never! 16 Do you not know that he who unites himself with a prostitute is one with her in body? For it is said, "The two will become one flesh." 17 But whoever is united with the Lord is one with him in spirit.

18 Flee from sexual immorality. All other sins a person commits are outside the body, but whoever sins sexually, sins against their own body. 19 Do you not know that your bodies are temples of the Holy Spirit, who is in you, whom you have received from God? You are not your own; 20 you were bought at a price. Therefore honor God with your bodies.

1 Corinthians 6:15–20

INTRODUCTION

God created everything out of nothing. There were no pre-existing materials He used in creating. He created man in His image, and there was nothing created that was not made by Him. He is separated from the created order. He is the supreme and sovereign God, as He has infinite power and total control over everything that He created. He is self- sufficient, as no part of creation is to be considered an extension of God.

He has called us into fellowship with Him through the Spirit of God that dwells in us, which came to us through the death of His Son, Jesus Christ. In His image, we are made to have the attributes of God and to have dominion over everything He has made. Living a holy life and walking in obedience to His commandments is one of the highest callings of mankind, enabling us to take charge of this earth and live a victorious life pleasing unto God.

Through the death of our Lord Jesus Christ, Christ has imputed His righteousness to us and has destroyed the strength of sin in us. He has called us to walk in holiness with Him. We ought to hold our bodies in high esteem, as God has made our bodies the dwelling place of the Holy Spirit, the third person of the Holy Trinity — God the Father, God the Son, and God the Holy Spirit. Our body is the temple where the Holy Spirit dwells, and we also honour Him with our body.

All thanks to God, who has come down to dwell with men. Hallelujah!

WE ARE FEARFULL AND WON-DERFULLY MADE

But you are a chosen people, a royal priesthood, a holy nation, God's special possession, that you may declare the praises of him who called you out of darkness into his wonderful light. (1 Peter 2:9)

We are created in the image of God to have God's attributes to be strong and powerful. God wants to work through us as individuals to bring blessings to all human life. From the beginning, God had always wanted a relationship with man, as this can be seen in the life of Adam and Eve before their fall when He came to fellow ship with them.

Then the man and his wife heard the sound of the LORD God as he was walking in the garden in the cool of the day, and they hid from the LORD God among the trees of the garden. But the LORD God called to the man, "Where are you?"(Genesis 3:8-9)

After the fall of the first Adam, God , through His Son Jesus Christ (the Second Adam), restored our fallen relationship with Him by reconciling us to Himself, not counting our trespasses against us. Through His grace and the death of His Son, we became the righteousness of God and vessels of honour unto Him. The Spirit of God came to dwell in man, making our body His dwelling place, unlike in the Old Testament, when His Spirit descended into the temple and upon a few individuals.

He created us to be fruitful, multiply, fill the earth, and subdue it. No human is superior to another. Man is not to rule or dominate another man but to complement each other and take dominion over everything else that God has created — to be caretakers and rulers over His creation. However, this is not the case today, as seen.

26 Then God said, "Let us make mankind in our image, in our likeness, so that they may rule over the fish in the sea and the birds in the sky, over the livestock and all the wild animals,[a] and over all the creatures that move along the ground." 27 So God created mankind in his own image, in the image of God he created them; male and female he created them. 28 God blessed them and said to them, "Be fruitful and increase in number; fill the earth and subdue it. Rule over the fish in the sea and the birds in the sky and over every living creature that moves on the ground." 29 Then God

said, "I give you every seed-bearing plant on the face of the whole earth and every tree that has fruit with seed in it. They will be yours for food. ³⁰ And to all the beasts of the earth and all the birds in the sky and all the creatures that move along the ground — everything that has the breath of life in it — I give every green plant for food." And it was so. ³¹ God saw all that he had made, and it was very good. And there was evening, and there was morning — the sixth day. (Genesis 1:26-31)

In this list, man was not mentioned as being controlled, but now the reverse is the case, as creation has taken control of some individuals. This is a result of the fallen nature of man, caused by sin and not identifying who we are.

Who are You?

It is a question that everyone will have to answer in order to help you fulfil your destiny and your purpose on earth. It is very important you identify who you are while living to fulfil your calling before it's too late because it is a question that you must know while living to fulfil your journey on earth. No one can escape it ; it's either we understand it now while living, or it will come to play on the day of reckoning when it will be revealed unto one for the purpose for which one was created. No man is here by chance or by accident. Jesus Christ, our saviour, has his own purpose too.

The one who does what is sinful is of the devil, because the devil has been sinning from the beginning. The reason the Son of God appeared was to destroy the devil's work. (1 John 3:8)

The earlier we discover who we are, the more we become fit as a vessel of honour in God's hand.

I pray for you that God, in His mercy, will help you discover who you are right here on earth so as to fulfil your destiny and purpose on earth in Jesus' name. Amen .

Sin has imprisoned man and reduced man to a pitiable situation of powerlessness. The Holy Spirit in a man is the only one that can reveal your true identity to you. This earth is not our destination; it does not hold our final residence, as a lot of times, people live as if this is their permanent residence and will live on earth forever. Let us stop living as if the earth is our permanent home. Earthly life is lost upon death, and we pass on to eternity. People store up treasures on earth, steal, prostitute, covet other people's wealth, kill, assassinate, and commit all kinds of vile acts just to acquire riches that are not eternal. Everything on earth is subject to decay, rust, and death.

19 "Do not store up for yourselves treasures on earth, where moths and vermin destroy, and where thieves break in and steal. 20 But store up for yourselves treasures in heaven, where moths and vermin do not destroy, and where thieves do not break in and steal. 21 For where your treasure is, there your heart will be also. (Matthew 6:19-21)

We are not here by accident. Neither are we here to occupy space and spend time on earth gallivanting. We are here to live a purposeful life and to fulfil our calling and destiny , not to copy someone else's life. You cannot find your true self and the power deposited in you by God , which makes you different and unique , by imitating others. We can imitate God's attributes and continue striving to live righteously, as this will help us in our destiny walk.

You must discover who you are, your purpose on earth, where exactly you are going, and what you will be remembered for when you are gone because when you are gone, your memory still lives on. We are not to live an unexamined life but to be intentional as wise children of God.

Be very careful, then, how you live — not as unwise but as wise. (Ephesians 5:15)

When you know who you are, you will know where you are going and that God is the only source that will take you to your destination. Knowing divinely who you are leads you to God. You will not go everywhere, as you will tread cautiously in order to fulfil your destiny. The greatest weapon of the enemy is to distract people so they do not live a fulfilled life. You will find your true self as you continue to seek the knowledge of knowing Him more. As you seek God, He will continue to renew and transform your life through His word , cleansing your sin and guilt through the atonement of the blood of Jesus and releasing your soul from the guilt of sin. God hates sin with perfect hatred. The devil, the father of all liars, is the fallen archangel, a rebel set to destroy men. One of his strongest holds on man is the sin of sexual immorality, which destroys the body of man and pollutes his mind so that man remains in perpetual transgression. The body, which is supposed to be the dwelling place of the Holy Spirit, is defiled so that man loses touch with God.

The body houses the spirit of man, which is supposed to be in direct contact with God. If the body, which is meant to house the spirit of man, is destroyed by sin, a man dies a premature death and will not be able to live and fulfil his destiny because sin has destroyed him and brought untimely death upon him. The most tragic outcome is the destruction of the temple within man, as the place of communion between the spirit of man and God becomes inaccessible, and man continues to live groping in darkness. Then, on the day of judgement, the devil will not be the only one condemned to eternal damnation.

Then he will say to those on his left, 'Depart from me, you who are cursed, into the eternal fire prepared for the devil and his an gels. (Matthew 25:41)

OUR SOURCE

We have all come from a source, and the source is God Al mighty, the self-sufficient one. As He has known Jeremiah, God has also known us beforehand. God knew beforehand who he was as a prophet to the nation. Jeremiah doubted at a point in his life whether he was really a prophet due to the Israelites' continuous disobedience to God's calls for repentance and the delay in God's judgment over their sin of idolatry.

God is our true source, and He is the one who can tell you who you are through the Spirit of God in YOU. And who the Holy Spirit says you are is who you are. Do not allow the voice in your head to tell you otherwise. This makes life easier for you and helps you focus on the blueprint of your calling so as to align with your divine purpose on earth and live a more fulfilling life. He had ordained and sanctified Jeremiah as a prophet even before he was conceived; likewise, YOU and I — He has called us into different ministries and careers that we need to pursue.

Before I formed you in the womb I knew[a] you, before you were born I set you apart; I appointed you as a prophet to the nations. (Jeremiah 1:5)

He has foreknown us and predestined us to be conformed to the image of His dear Son.

Knowing who you are and your mission on earth is a spiritual journey you must be willing to undertake in order to discover the secret in the spiritual realm, hidden from your physical eyes and human understanding, as we continue to seek God in the Spirit. As you seek God in spirit and in truth, you will receive revelation and understanding with the power of becoming your original, true version, even as you continue to walk in the Spirit.

THERE IS NO OTHER GOD BESIDES GOD ALMIGHTY

There is no other God besides Him. He made all things, and there is no other like Him. He alone has created the heaven of heavens, the earth, and the seas, and there was nothing made that was not created by Him.

10 "You are my witnesses," declares the Lord, "and my servant whom I have chosen, so that you may know and believe me and understand that I am he. Before me no god was formed, nor will there be one after me. 11 I, even I, am the Lord, and apart from me there is no savior. (Isaiah 43:10-11)

The devil does not want us to discover who we are because identifying your true self is one of the surest ways of finding God. He has made men believe there are other gods. As we see in the world today, different kinds of gods are being worshipped — the stars, the moon, the sun, and even handmade wooden artistic work created by man etc. This truth the devil has cleverly concealed from men so they will endlessly continue to search for other gods in vain and for solutions to their needs, which they will never find because there is no other saviour able to save besides God.

Salvation is found in no one else, for there is no other name under heaven given to mankind by which we must be saved. (Acts 4:12)

Pharaoh, with all the magicians and idols that he had around him, couldn't save himself. Even the plague of darkness , which was the ninth plague he was afflicted with — darkness in Egypt for three days — being considered the "son of Re ," which means "son of the sun ," the sun never came to his rescue to give him light , nor did the other gods he worshipped. Every plague that came upon them represented the symbol of one god or another that the Egyptians worshipped, yet they all went to sleep and couldn't save him. God is the only one who can truly save.

21 Then the Lord said to Moses, "Stretch out your hand toward the sky so that darkness spreads over Egypt — darkness that can be felt. 22 So Moses stretched out his hand toward the sky, and total darkness covered all Egypt for three days. 23 No one could see any one else or move about for three days. Yet all the Israelites had light in the places where they lived. (Exodus 10:21-23)

There are many instances in the Bible where men have trusted their idols , and at the end of the day, those idols have disappointed and failed them. Today, some people are still making the same mistake. The foolishness of man in trusting manmade idols can be seen more in-depth in this passage of the Bible, which has shown how idols have failed men from generation to generation.

[8] Do not tremble, do not be afraid. Did I not proclaim this and foretell it long ago? You are my witnesses. Is there any God besides me? No, there is no other Rock; I know not one. [9] All who make idols are nothing, and the things they treasure are worthless. Those who would speak up for them are blind; they are ignorant, to their own shame. [10] Who shapes a god and casts an idol, which can profit nothing? [11] People who do that will be put to shame; such crafts men are only human beings. Let them all come together and take their stand; they will be brought down to terror and shame. [12] The blacksmith takes a tool and works with it in the coals; he shapes an idol with hammers, he forges it with the might of his arm. He gets hungry and loses his strength; he drinks no water and grows faint. [13] The carpenter measures with a line and makes an outline with a marker; he roughs it out with chisels and marks it with com passes. He shapes it in human form, human form in all its glory,

that it may dwell in a shrine. ¹⁴ He cut down cedars, or perhaps took a cypress or oak. He let it grow among the trees of the forest, or planted a pine, and the rain made it grow. ¹⁵ It is used as fuel for burning; some of it he takes and warms himself, he kindles a fire and bakes bread. But he also fashions a god and worships it; he makes an idol and bows down to it. ¹⁶ Half of the wood he burns in the fire; over it he prepares his meal, he roasts his meat and eats his fill. He also warms himself and says, "Ah! I am warm; I see the fire." ¹⁷ From the rest he makes a god, his idol; he bows down to it and worships. He prays to it and says, "Save me! You are my god!" ¹⁸ They know nothing, they understand nothing; their eyes are plastered over so they cannot see, and their minds closed so they cannot understand. ¹⁹ No one stops to think, no one has the knowledge or understanding to say, "Half of it I used for fuel; I even baked bread over its coals, I roasted meat and I ate. Shall I make a detestable thing from what is left? Shall I bow down to a block of wood?" (Isaiah 44:8-19)

The image of God, made by man , has to be carried by man, and the man falls and worships it, builds a house for it, and says, "Deliver me ." Satan has shut their eyes so they cannot see and their hearts so they cannot understand. He possesses them by his evil spirit to make man believe there are other gods. He has deceived them lest they know the truth and turn to the one and only true God.

The Lord commanded that we should not make any graven images...

No one should ascribe the power of redemption to any god other than God Almighty.

He is not just the God of Israel but of the entire nation.

No matter how clever, intelligent, or hardworking a person might be, good success flows only from the gracious hand of God.

The devil has tricked men into believing that there are other gods because he knows that if men should know the truth — that the Lord alone is God and there is none besides Him — they will seek Him. The Eternal Rock of Ages, the only true and living God, the Almighty One. And when they find Him, they will find their true selves. They will be delivered from problems and challenges that have come upon them as a result of sin .

[18] And we all, who with unveiled faces contemplate[a] the Lord's glory, are being transformed into his image with ever-increasing glory, which comes from the Lord, who is the Spirit. (2

Corinthians 3:18)

**The Lord has blinded their eyes and hardened their hearts —
so that their eyes cannot see, and their hearts cannot understand,
and they cannot turn to me and have me heal them. (John 12:40)**

Living in this ignorance cannot help you to fulfil your destiny
and your true calling on earth. You will live quite alright, but it
wouldn't be to your highest calling. Some people are living and run-
ning in another person's lane without knowledge of it, and even
when it seems they have won in that lane, it does not make them a
winner or make it right. In failing to know his source and obtain the
blueprint of his life, many lives have been ruined and wasted, and
some are hanging by a thin thread. Some have succeeded, but not
in Christ, and the supposed success has brought sorrow upon them.

**Keep this Book of the Law always on your lips; meditate on it
day and night, so that you may be careful to do everything written
in it. Then you will be prosperous and successful. (Joshua 1:8)**

Man has given a lot of preference to creatures that were created
by God and has even stooped so low as to worship them rather than
the Creator. A lot of people are spiritually blinded by the glamorous

18

things the world can offer, without thinking twice about the consequences — the consequences which are greater than the temporary result or pleasure. Men have degraded themselves to a pitiable position by living in sin and engaging in all kinds of sexual immorality because they feel they have the right to do so , using a common cliché that is very popular: "It's my body ," "It's my life," "It's my business ," and "I can do whatsoever I choose to do with it ." None of us lives to ourselves, and none dies to himself; we are to present our bodies as a living sacrifice to the Lord. We live, and we die in Christ. We will all give an account of our stewardship to God for the lives we live on earth, even for every word we speak. Your body is more sacred than you can ever imagine because we are the redeemed of the Lord. He gave up His life that we may live. We are saved by the blood that was shed on the cross of Calvary by our Saviour.

If we live, we live for the Lord; and if we die, we die for the Lord. So, whether we live or die, we belong to the Lord. (Romans 14:8)

It's not your life — you shall give an account of your life. Your life is also connected to other people's destinies, so be very careful and do not be blinded by selfishness. You are not here to live for yourself alone but to touch the lives connected to you in a positive way. Some people do not respect or regard their bodies as the dwelling place of the Holy Spirit and have resorted to degrading their bodies into tents of all manner of wickedness and sexual perversion. This act has destroyed lives and cut short the promising futures of young people at the peak of their lives , depriving them of the chance to know who they are.

We shall not die without fulfilling our destiny, singing our song, and being celebrated, in Jesus' name, Amen.

We must impart the world positively and serve God with all our strength, might, and love. That is the basic reason why you are here — to be the light of the world so that men may see you and your good deeds and praise God. You must live a legacy that will outlive you, bringing generational blessings, and not leave behind burdens and curses for your unborn generations.

Reuben was the first born of Jacob. According to the custom of Israel in those days, the firstborn always enjoyed a double portion of the inheritance, but Reuben lost it as he committed the sin of sexual immorality with his father's wife. Rather than a double portion of inheritance, he was cursed by his father with the words, "Thou shall not excel." From the topmost position of "the excellency of dignity and the excellency of power ," he fell to the bottom. He lost all his rulership and kingship to his brother Judah because he could not control his sexual desire.

³ Reuben, you are my firstborn, my might, the first sign of my strength, excelling in honor, excelling in power. ⁴ Turbulent as the waters, you will no longer excel, for you went up onto your father's bed, onto my couch and defiled it. (Genesis 49:3-4)

Prayer Point

Confess your sin, both the one you have committed intentionally and unknowingly, to God and ask for His mercy in Jesus' name. Amen.

Ask God to open your eyes to see His glory, your ears to hear, and your mind to understand, that you may know the truth that will set you free in Jesus' name. Amen.

Ask God to show you who you are — your original self — and for the Holy Spirit to help you become what He has created you to be in Jesus' name. Amen.

THE ALTAR AND TEMPLE BUILT BY MEN

In the Old Testament, men, in their hunger and thirst for God, have found Him, as some seek Him earnestly, and to some men, God has appeared in theophany . To others, He has spoken one -on -one, like Moses. Most of them, at the point of their encounter where God revealed Himself to them , built an altar as a place of worship or a memorial of their encounter. For every altar, temple, and church to stand, there must be an act of instruction from God and obedience from men.

In the Old Testament, the Spirit of God had not yet come to dwell with men, but God always came down to man and over shadowed him with His presence in order for him to carry out a specific assignment . An example is the building of the Tabernacle of God, as God instructed Moses to go to Bezalel , upon whom His Spirit rested. The skills required to do the work were given to him and the others who would join him in executing the task.

31 The Lord said to Moses, 2 "See, I have called by name Bezalel the son of Uri, son of Hur, of the tribe of Judah, 3 and I have filled

him with the Spirit of God, with ability and intelligence, with knowledge and all craftsmanship, 4 to devise artistic designs, to work in gold, silver, and bronze, 5 in cutting stones for setting, and in carving wood, to work in every craft. 6 And behold, I have appointed with him Oholiab, the son of Ahisamach, of the tribe of Dan. And I have given to all able men ability, that they may make all that I have commanded you. (Exodus 31:1–6)

These great men of God built an altar for Him. Abraham was one of those who had an encounter with God that changed his life. He had a covenant of circumcision — a covenant that Abraham had to keep between himself and his descendants, as every male child had to be circumcised. It was an outward physical sign of an eternal relationship between God and the Israelites as His chosen people.

The removal of the flesh of the foreskin, which he abided by in faith, meant that he was circumcised at the age of 90 years to show his willingness to submit himself entirely to God. This was a fore shadowing of what was yet to come in the New Testament when grace would be put to work instead of the law — that through the death of Jesus Christ, we would receive the Spirit of God, and the law of God would be written in our hearts. We would be redeemed from the power of sin through the law and adopted as sons of God. In this dispensation of grace, brought about by the death of Jesus Christ, we became the temple of God, not built by hands but fashioned by the Holy Spirit of God.

25 Circumcision has value if you observe the law, but if you break the law, you have become as though you had not been circumcised. 26 So then, if those who are not circumcised keep the law's requirements, will they not be regarded as though they were circumcised? 27 The one who is not circumcised physically and yet obeys the law will condemn you who, even though you have the[a] written code and circumcision, are a lawbreaker. 28 A person is not a Jew who is one only outwardly, nor is circumcision merely out

ward and physical. 29 No, a person is a Jew who is one inwardly; and circumcision is circumcision of the heart, by the Spirit, not by the written code. Such a person's praise is not from other people, but from God. (Romans 2:25-29)

Moses was one of the prophets of God, the only one with whom God communicated face-to-face . At that time, the Spirit of God had not yet come to dwell in man. God instructed Moses to build a tabernacle. You need to see the specifications given by God to Moses for building the temple from **Exodus 25** through **Exodus 27** The heaviness of the temple curtain in the New Testament, according to the Mishnah, was described as follows: '*It was 60 feet long, 30 feet wide, and as thick as a man's palm, requiring 300 men to lift it when wet.*' This curtain was torn from top to bottom, veiling the sanctuary and the Holy of Holies as Jesus Christ died on the cross of Calvary.

This temple was a shadow of things to come . Reading from **Exodus**, you can see how God prepared His people . Only the High Priest was allowed to go beyond the veil once a year after offering a sin sacrifice, even for himself. Now, Jesus Christ, our superior High Priest, sacrificed

Himself, and through His death, He created access for us to come to God . He became our High Priest.

The tabernacle was the forerunner of the temple that would be built by King Solomon, as God wanted to dwell among His people. The Ark of God, which symbolised His presence, was placed in the central part of the tabernacle. The building of the tabernacle was sa

cred, as God selected those who would construct it, down to the materials to be used.

After the construction of the tabernacle, Moses granted his brother Aaron and his descendants the priesthood, as they were set apart to serve God as part of the law received at Sinai. Aaron was the first chief priest of God. He was anointed and consecrated as commanded by God to be the mediator between the people and God. And God commanded that at the door of the tabernacle of the congregation, there should be a continuous burnt offering before the Lord throughout all generations, where the Lord would meet him.

[42] "For the generations to come this burnt offering is to be made regularly at the entrance to the tent of meeting, before the Lord. There I will meet you and speak to you; [43] there also I will meet with the Israelites, and the place will be consecrated by my glory. [44] "So I will consecrate the tent of meeting and the altar and will consecrate Aaron and his sons to serve me as priests. [45] Then I will dwell among the Israelites and be their God. [46] They will know that I am the Lord their God, who brought them out of Egypt so that I might dwell among them. I am the Lord their God. (Exodus 29:42- 46)

An altar was also built to burn incense, and there had to be a perpetual burning of fire continuously, non-stop. This is the same expectation of believers — to live righteously. The fire on your altar should never be extinguished but should keep burning continually as a sweet-smelling savour unto God, as His purifying fire continues to refine you.

In atonement for sin, the priest had a crucial role to play by sacrificing an animal and placing the animal's blood in the sanctuary. The more profound the impact of sin, the further into the tent the blood had to be applied — that is, the closer to the presence of the Lord, symbolised by the Ark. The rest of the blood was poured at the base of the altar in the courtyard to show that the individual's life belonged to God. This tabernacle , signifying the presence of God , wandered from tribe to tribe. The temple was meant to harbour God's presence despite the fact that neither heaven nor earth could contain Him.

I have not dwelt in a house from the day I brought the Israelites up out of Egypt to this day. I have been moving from place to place with a tent as my dwelling. (2 Samuel 7:6)

Afterwards, King Solomon built a temple for the Lord, replacing the tabernacle, and there was now a permanent residence for the temple of God. The Levites no longer had to carry the tabernacle and its equipment as they travelled from place to place. Now, with the birth of Jesus Christ, we carry the presence of God within us as individuals. We no longer need a proxy or a priest to cleanse us — we are built with no physical hands.

JESUS CHRIST AND THE NEW COVENANT

Jesus Christ is the only begotten Son of God , who was prophesied by the prophets in the Old and New Testament concerning His birth, death, and resurrection. The one (Messiah) that will come and save the world from the grip of darkness and deliver His people from the power of sin. He will conquer death and deliver the dead saints, as death will not hold Him bound.

For you will not abandon my soul to Sheol, nor will you let your holy one see corruption. (Psalm 16:10)

He is sinless, without blemish, being birthed by a virgin who was overshadowed by the Holy Ghost, as prophesied by Angel Gabriel.

26 In the sixth month of Elizabeth's pregnancy, God sent the angel Gabriel to Nazareth, a town in Galilee, 27 to a virgin pledged to be married to a man named Joseph, a descendant of David. The virgin's name was Mary. 28 The angel went to her and said, "Greetings, you who are highly favored! The Lord is with you." 29 Mary

was greatly troubled at his words and wondered what kind of greeting this might be. [30] But the angel said to her, "Do not be afraid, Mary; you have found favor with God. [31] You will conceive and give birth to a son, and you are to call him Jesus. [32] He will be great and will be called the Son of the Most High. The Lord God will give him the throne of his father David, [33] and he will reign over Jacob's descendants forever; his kingdom will never end." [34] "How will this be," Mary asked the angel, "since I am a virgin?"[35] The angel answered, "The Holy Spirit will come on you, and the power of the Most High will overshadow you. So the holy one to be born will be called the Son of God. (Luke 1:26-35)

Jesus Christ laid a new covenant for us, as He has not come to destroy the Law of Moses . We were kept in custody under the law until the promise that was once hidden would be revealed. Through Him, by faith, we are called the righteousness of God, as the law does not make us righteous. And as many that believe in Him are saved. God freely gave the world His only begotten Son in order to provide forgiveness for sin through the sacrificial blood of our Lord Jesus Christ on the cross of Calvary, and altogether, this reveals God's love for sinners.

²⁸ The priest is to make atonement before the Lord for the one who erred by sinning unintentionally, and when atonement has been made, that person will be forgiven. ²⁹ One and the same law applies to everyone who sins unintentionally, whether a native born Israelite or a foreigner residing among you. ³⁰ "'But anyone who sins defiantly, whether native-born or foreigner, blasphemes the Lord and must be cut off from the people of Israel. ³¹ Because they have despised the Lord's word and broken his commands, they must surely be cut off; their guilt remains on them.'" (Numbers 15:28-31)

The law was unable to deal with presumptuous sin but could atone for sins committed ignorantly. The law was given in or der to prepare us for the future by giving us an in-depth knowledge of who God is, what Jesus Christ did for us, and the price of our sin , which cost Him His life so that we may enjoy the new covenant of reconciliation with God the Father, as our sin has created a chasm and separated us from Him.

By Mosaic Law , cursed is anyone who hangs on a tree. God made Him, who is without sin, to be cursed for our sake and to bear the sin of the whole world in order for those who believe in Him to be saved and to receive the Abrahamic blessing.

¹³ Christ redeemed us from the curse of the law by becoming a curse for us, for it is written: "Cursed is everyone who is hung on a pole." ¹⁴ He redeemed us in order that the blessing given to Abraham might come to the Gentiles through Christ Jesus, so that by faith we might receive the promise of the Spirit. (Galatians 3:13- 14)

On the cross of Calvary, the Son of God became sin on our behalf and, as an offering for sin, He condemned sin in His flesh. Through the blood shed on the cross of Calvary , propitiation was made for each and every one of us. He became an atonement for our sin once and for all and imputed righteousness in us, which the law could not do, as cleansing was done by the high priest through the blood of an animal.

Thank You, Father, for the death of Jesus Christ on the cross of Calvary in order to set me free from sin . His death on the cross of Calvary shall not be in vain for me, in Jesus' name. Amen.

His death tore the curtain veil of the temple in Jerusalem. He became both the priest and the sacrifice as He entered into the Holy of Holies, which was the throne in Heaven, right before His Father, and made atonement for us once and for all into eternity. He created access and liberty for us and took us into the Holy of Holies.

The Holy of Holies was the innermost and most sacred place of the ancient Tabernacle of Moses, where the Ark of the Covenant was kept. It was only accessible by the high priest. We are no longer bound to the old covenant , where the priest made atonement for us and for his own sin with the blood of an animal once a year . Now, we all have full access to God the Father in the heavenly realm. Hallelujah ! Our God is good. Even the veil that covered our eyes and minds by the devil was torn, and we could see the light and be transformed into His image. We are no longer like those whose eyes have been blinded by the gods of this world.

The god of this age has blinded the minds of unbelievers, so that they cannot see the light of the gospel that displays the glory of Christ, who is the image of God. (2 Corinthians 4:4)

Through the law, sin was made known to us , helping us to see and understand the attributes of God as a just and holy God.

We have been cleansed once and for all by the blood of Jesus Christ and ransomed through His blood by God the Father. Now, in Christ Jesus, we who were once far away have been brought near by the blood of Jesus. Jesus Christ reconciled us to God through the cross, thereby putting the strength of sin to death. We are called to walk in unity as one body, one spirit, one faith, one Lord, one baptism, one God and Father of all, who is above all, and through all, and in us all.

¹⁴ having canceled the charge of our legal indebtedness, which stood against us and condemned us; he has taken it away, nailing it to the cross. ¹⁵ And having disarmed the powers and authorities, he made a public spectacle of them, triumphing over them by the cross. (Colossians 2 :14 –15)

THE NEW TEMPLE IN US

In the Old Testament, one of the presumptions of the pre-exilic people was that God dwelt in the temple. They believed that God lived in their midst, and no matter how much they were warned by the prophet to change their ways and turn back to God so as not to go into captivity, they did not hearken to them. They felt that no matter how disobedient they were, they could never be taken into captivity.

This attitude had no justification, as King Solomon made it clear to them in order to persuade them to live a life of obedience — to honour, obey, and fear God, and to live a life of total submission, obedience, and humility.

"But will God really dwell on earth? The heavens, even the highest heaven, cannot contain you. How much less this temple I have built! (1 Kings 8:27)

King Solomon built the temple in Jerusalem, and after the destruction of the temple by Nebuchadnezzar, the king of Babylon , there was a negative attitude during its rebuilding, as they said the temple would be inferior to Solomon's temple , which was covered with gold .

2 The temple that King Solomon built for the Lord was sixty cubits long, twenty wide and thirty high.[a] 3 The portico at the front of the main hall of the temple extended the width of the temple, that is twenty cubits,[b] and projected ten cubits[c] from the front of the temple. 4 He made narrow windows high up in the temple walls. 5 Against the walls of the main hall and inner sanctuary he built a structure around the building, in which there were side rooms. 6 The lowest floor was five cubits[d] wide, the middle floor six cubits[e] and the third floor seven.[f] He made offset ledges around the outside of the temple so that nothing would be inserted into the temple walls.

7 In building the temple, only blocks dressed at the quarry were used, and no hammer, chisel or any other iron tool was heard at the temple site while it was being built.

8 The entrance to the lowest[g] floor was on the south side of the temple; a stairway led up to the middle level and from there to the third. 9 So he built the temple and completed it, roofing it with beams and cedar planks. 10 And he built the side rooms all along the temple. The height of each was five cubits, and they were attached to the temple by beams of cedar.

[11] The word of the Lord came to Solomon: [12] "As for this temple you are building, if you follow my decrees, observe my laws and keep all my commands and obey them, I will fulfill through you the promise I gave to David your father. [13] And I will live among the Israelites and will not abandon my people Israel."

[14] So Solomon built the temple and completed it. [15] He lined its interior walls with cedar boards, paneling them from the floor of the temple to the ceiling, and covered the floor of the temple with planks of juniper. [16] He partitioned off twenty cubits at the rear of the temple with cedar boards from floor to ceiling to form within the temple an inner sanctuary, the Most Holy Place. [17] The main hall in front of this room was forty cubits[h] long. [18] The inside of the temple was cedar, carved with gourds and open flowers. Everything was cedar; no stone was to be seen.

[19] He prepared the inner sanctuary within the temple to set the ark of the covenant of the Lord there. [20] The inner sanctuary was twenty cubits long, twenty wide and twenty high. He overlaid the inside with pure gold, and he also overlaid the altar of cedar. [21]

Solomon covered the inside of the temple with pure gold, and he extended gold chains across the front of the inner sanctuary, which was overlaid with gold. [22] So he overlaid the whole interior with gold. He also overlaid with gold the altar that belonged to the inner sanctuary.

23 For the inner sanctuary he made a pair of cherubim out of olive wood, each ten cubits high. 24 One wing of the first cherub was five cubits long, and the other wing five cubits — ten cubits from wing tip to wing tip. 25 The second cherub also measured ten cubits, for the two cherubim were identical in size and shape. 26 The height of each cherub was ten cubits. 27 He placed the cherubim inside the innermost room of the temple, with their wings spread out. The wing of one cherub touched one wall, while the wing of the other touched the other wall, and their wings touched each other in the middle of the room. 28 He overlaid the cherubim with gold.

29 On the walls all around the temple, in both the inner and outer rooms, he carved cherubim, palm trees and open flowers. 30 He also covered the floors of both the inner and outer rooms of the temple with gold.

31 For the entrance to the inner sanctuary he made doors out of olive wood that were one fifth of the width of the sanctuary. 32 And on the two olive-wood doors he carved cherubim, palm trees and open flowers, and overlaid the cherubim and palm trees with

hammered gold. [33] In the same way, for the entrance to the main hall he made doorframes out of olive wood that were one fourth of the width of the hall. [34] He also made two doors out of juniper wood, each having two leaves that turned in sockets. 35 He carved cherubim, palm trees and open flowers on them and overlaid them with gold hammered evenly over the carvings. (1 Kings 6:2-35)

God was providing restoration and cleansing through a glorious temple and a messianic ruler , Jesus Christ, and we were assured that the glory of this latter house shall be greater than the glory of the former .

'The glory of this present house will be greater than the glory of the former house,' says the Lord Almighty. 'And in this place I will grant peace,' declares the Lord Almighty." (Haggai 2:9)

Jesus is the builder and the finisher of the complete work of God's true house , and He shall reign forever as His kingdom shall have no end.

And I tell you that you are Peter, and on this rock I will build my church, and the gates of Hades will not overcome it. (Matthew 16:18)

We bear the spirit of God, and all the powers of hell cannot conquer us. We cannot be plundered like the old temple by our enemies, in Jesus' name. Amen. Through Jesus Christ, born of the Virgin Mary, as prophesied by Isaiah , He shall be named Emmanuel, meaning " God with us ." God has come to dwell among His people in a perfect relationship of holiness, which has always been His desire . When we worship Him properly and put our trust in Him , He will forgive all sinners who repent and return to Him.

An unregenerated person living before Christ and Pentecost did not have the permanent and empowering gift of the Holy Spirit. The spirit of God now lives in us as believers; the Lord reigns over all. Worshipping Him is not limited to just a physical house or a geographical location — you can find Him within you when you abide in Him, and He abides in you, too. Just as the church is the body of Christ, a holy, undefiled church, so are you in Christ Jesus.

[48] "However, the Most High does not live in houses made by human hands. As the prophet says: [49] "'Heaven is my throne, and the earth is my footstool. What kind of house will you build for me? says the Lord. Or where will my resting place be? [50] Has not my hand made all these things?' (Acts 7:48-50)

We need to take our walk with God seriously. The tent was a special place for the ark, and the priests offered their sacrifices there, but now the new temple is in you.

21 "Woman," Jesus replied, "believe me, a time is coming when you will worship the Father neither on this mountain nor in Jerusalem. 22 You Samaritans worship what you do not know; we worship what we do know, for salvation is from the Jews. 23 Yet a time is coming and has now come when the true worshipers will worship the Father in the Spirit and in truth, for they are the kind of worshipers the Father seeks. 24 God is spirit, and his worshipers must worship in the Spirit and in truth." (John 4:21-24)

The great work wrought by our forefathers when the spirit of God had not yet come to dwell with man shows us how much more we can achieve now that the spirit resides within us as we walk in righteousness and obedience to God. We shall be strong and do exploits in Jesus' name. Amen.

20 Once, on being asked by the Pharisees when the kingdom of God would come, Jesus replied, "The coming of the kingdom of God is not something that can be observed, 21 nor will people say, 'Here it is,' or 'There it is,' because the kingdom of God is in your midst." (Luke 17:20-21)

Jesus is the hope of the promise made by God to our fathers. We have to trust God and surrender to His authority, even when we cannot make sense of the circumstances, as His ways are higher than our ways.

As the heavens are higher than the earth, so are my ways higher than your ways and my thoughts than your thoughts. (Isaiah 55:9)

As we walk in obedience, the truth will be revealed to us. He is our physical and spiritual deliverer. He moves in mysterious ways.

For the wisdom of this world is foolishness in God's sight. As it is written: "He catches the wise in their craftiness" (1 Corinthians 3:19)

THE HOLY SPIRIT IN A MAN

The Holy Spirit makes provision for us as a Comforter, Counsellor, Helper, Intercessor, Advocate, Strengthener, and standby. The Holy Spirit convicts us of our sins and shows us how we have fallen away from the truth to lead us into repentance and not go astray.

When he comes, he will prove the world to be in the wrong about sin and righteousness and judgment: John 16:8

Man is a spirit that dwells in the body with the soul. Our spirit is made to connect with the Spirit of God , which brings all truth to us and helps us live a fulfilled life — not just as a mere man but as a spiritual being. However, sin in man has made that impossible and has disconnected man from the original plan of God. As a result, man has lived a carnal life (life in the flesh) and is powerless, for to be carnally minded is death, even while living. The world has subjected man to live by intellectual knowledge and emotions rather than through the spirit , which connects man to God for super intelligence and revelation of the kingdom mysteries that will help him live a supernatural life. The Spirit of God unleashes power in us, as

He did not give us the spirit of fear but of power, love, and a sound mind.

As children of God and born again, we are now born of God.

Children born not of natural descent, nor of human decision or a husband's will, but born of God. John 1:13

He has beckoned us to come to Him — all of us who are heavy -laden — and He will give us rest, as His anointing shall break every yoke and lift away every burden . This anointing comes to us through the Holy Spirit , bringing ease into our lives. The Holy Spirit ignites the fire of God in our lives and sets the altar of God in our hearts on fire. It is very important for a child of God to be imbued with the Holy Spirit. Without it, we can do nothing. The world will toss us up and down, as it favours those who know where they are going and the God that they serve. The Holy Spirit is your compass and guide in life. For a righteous believer with the indwelling of the Holy Spirit, you will bear fruit and be productive.

7 If you remain in me and my words remain in you, ask whatever you wish, and it will be done for you. 8 This is to my Father's glory, that you bear much fruit, showing yourselves to be my disciples.

9 "As the Father has loved me, so have I loved you. Now remain in my love. 10 If you keep my commands, you will remain in my love, just as I have kept my Father's commands and remain in his love. 11 I have told you this so that my joy may be in you and that your joy may be complete. 12 My command is this: Love each other as I have loved you. 13 Greater love has no one than this: to lay down one's life for one's friends. 14 You are my friends if you do what I command. 15 I no longer call you servants, because a servant does not know his master's business. Instead, I have called you friends, for everything that I learned from my Father I have made known to you. 16 You did not choose me, but I chose you and appointed you so that you might go and bear fruit — fruit that will last — and so that whatever you ask in my name the Father will give you. (John 15:7-16)

It is pathetic that we don't know the power that has been bestowed on us as children of God — to be called sons and daughters of the Highest. In the time of Elisha, the Spirit of God came and went, yet he did great exploits and demonstrated immense spiritual power. He shared prophetic messages with his ungodly king as God showed him mercy to deliver His people from the warring king of Syria. At one point, the Syrian king thought there was a spy among them who reported their plans to the king of Israel — an offence that attracted capital punishment for treason.

"None of us, my lord the king," said one of his officers, "but Elisha, the prophet who is in Israel, tells the king of Israel the very words you speak in your bedroom." (2 Kings 6:12)

These were great seekers of God whose passion brought down God's glory upon them, allowing them to perform great miracles. How much more now that we have the Spirit living right inside of us? Yet, many Christians are defeated by their enemies, walking straight into traps without so much as batting an eyelid because they have eyes but do not see ears that do not hear, and hearts that are waxed cold and cannot perceive.

Hear this, you foolish and senseless people, who have eyes but do not see, who have ears but do not hear: (Jeremiah 5:21)

Let us boast in Christ, through whom the world has been crucified to us, making us new creatures as we live in obedience to God. The Spirit of God in man is the temple, not built by hands. No one can say , "Jesus is Lord," except by the Holy Spirit. Now, as believers , let us not grieve the Holy Spirit in us by being disobedient to the word of God and the voice of the Holy Spirit. Al ways be right with your conscience so as not to short -change yourself of the blessings that come from God through the Spirit of truth. The Spirit allows the light of God to illuminate your heart and reveals the knowledge of the glory of God. We do not look at things as they appear at face value, for through the Spirit, we see things for what they truly represent. The natural man does not receive the things of the Spirit of God, for they are foolishness to him, nor can he know them, for they are spiritually discerned. We have the mind of Christ. He will destroy the wisdom of the wise and bring to nothing the understanding of the prudent.

We must dedicate ourselves totally to God , living in holiness by offering our bodies to Him as living sacrifices and dwelling places for the Holy Spirit , for the Spirit of God does not dwell in a filthy vessel. God is less concerned about constructing holy places of worship than He is about people having holy hearts, making them dwelling places for the Spirit of God.

"Woman," Jesus replied, "believe me, a time is coming when you will worship the Father neither on this mountain nor in Jerusalem. (John 4:21)

He wants us to act as legitimate children of God , as true worshippers who worship Him in truth and spirit, and to act justly towards one another. It is not just about the right place of worship but also the state of mind of the worshipper — holiness within and without. Jesus Christ spoke in parables to the religious leaders, yet they failed to understand Him when He said, "Destroy this temple, and in three days, I will raise it up." They replied, "It took forty-six years to build the temple; how can He rebuild it in three days?"

Jesus answered them, "Destroy this temple, and I will raise it again in three days." (John 2:19)

Unknown to them , He was referring to His body — the temple of His body — His death and resurrection, which has now spread abroad to us , making us conformable to His death and establishing His invisible temple within us. This is proof that our bodies are the temples of God. Christ is not preached by the wisdom of this world.

For the message of the cross is foolishness to those who are perishing, but to us who are being saved it is the power of God. (1 Corinthians 1:18)

For the Holy Spirit to dwell in you, you must be born of water and the Spirit, not of the flesh , for that which is born of the flesh is flesh. A new birth in Christ brings a regenerated heart. We must be born again to live and walk in the Spirit, as God will continue to conform us to the image of our Lord Jesus Christ so that we do not walk in the flesh.

The works of the flesh are evident: sexual immorality, envy, maliciousness, impurity, idolatry, jealousy, strife, fits of anger, rivalries, division, drunkenness, orgies, dissensions, enmity, witchcraft, selfish ambition, debauchery, hatred, lust, pride, un cleanness, heresies, and the like. The Spirit of God does not dwell in such a body. No good thing dwells in the flesh, as the flesh always seeks pleasure for the physical body without regard for the soul and spirit . It desires everything contrary to the Spirit and lacks character and self-control. This is the state of a carnal man because he walks in the flesh and not in the Spirit, as spiritual things seem foolish to him. The flesh has only one thing to offer : death to an unrepentant soul.

"It is the Spirit who gives life, and when you walk in the Spirit, you will not fulfil the lust of the flesh ." If you are led by the Spirit, you will not lust after the flesh, for the flesh profits nothing. The word of God is Spirit and life to believers. We die to sin to be alive in Christ through the power of His resurrection so we may walk in the Spirit.

16 So I say, walk by the Spirit, and you will not gratify the desires of the flesh. 17 For the flesh desires what is contrary to the

Spirit, and the Spirit what is contrary to the flesh. They are in conflict with each other, so that you are not to do whatever[a] you want. [18] But if you are led by the Spirit, you are not under the law.

[19] The acts of the flesh are obvious: sexual immorality, impurity and debauchery; [20] idolatry and witchcraft; hatred, discord, jealousy, fits of rage, selfish ambition, dissensions, factions [21] and envy; drunkenness, orgies, and the like. I warn you, as I did before, that those who live like this will not inherit the kingdom of God.

[22] But the fruit of the Spirit is love, joy, peace, forbearance, kindness, goodness, faithfulness, [23] gentleness and self-control. Against such things there is no law. (Galatians 5:16-23)

His grace is sufficient for us . If we live in the Spirit, let us also walk in the Spirit. Let us not provoke one another or envy one another. Invite the Holy Spirit into your life after your prayer of repentance and believe in the Word of God. Trust in the Lord with all your strength and lean not on your own understanding. Having believed, we are sealed by the Holy Spirit. He made us alive,

who were once dead in trespasses and sins , according to the prince of the power of the air, fulfilling the desires of the flesh and mind.

God, in His mercy, has shown us mercy.

⁴ **But because of his great love for us, God, who is rich in mercy,** ⁵ **made us alive with Christ even when we were dead in transgressions — it is by grace you have been saved.** ⁶ **And God raised us up with Christ and seated us with him in the heavenly realms in Christ Jesus,** ⁷ **in order that in the coming ages he might show the incomparable riches of his grace, expressed in his kindness to us in Christ Jesus.** ⁸ **For it is by grace you have been saved, through faith — and this is not from yourselves, it is the gift of God —** ⁹ **not by works, so that no one can boast. (Ephesians 2:4-9)**

The Levites provided a visible presence among the 12 tribes to remind them of the need for holiness and the righteousness of God. Today, we have the Holy Spirit to help us with all things , to respond to 's love with loving obedience and not fearful obedience. Without the Holy Spirit, as believers, we cannot do anything. Jesus Christ was a stalwart to His disciples during the time He was physically present on earth. The Holy Spirit is now our standby power of God , released to a believer today.

The life of a believer is encoded and entwined in the Spirit, too. You must balance it with the physical to live a victorious life and experience freedom and breakthroughs in the earthly realm.

Flesh gives birth to flesh, but the Spirit gives birth to spirit. (John 3:6)

ACTIONS TO TAKE IN ORDER TO KEEP YOUR TEMPLE BURNING

Stay away from all appearances of sin and sexual immorality

Sexual immorality is a sin against 's body, assaulting the sanctity of a believer's sacred oneness with Christ, the Holy Spirit in you, and the oneness of holy matrimony between Jesus Christ and man that made us His bride.

The believer's body is a sacred vessel. We have been ransomed and bought by the blood of Jesus Christ, the Son of God. We have no business doing anything with the L's body that does not glorify God. We have to be holy, as without holiness, no one can see God — holiness within and without. Resist the devil, and he will flee from you. When we resist the devil, he takes flight away from us. Although atrando (m, he might make a comeback — that's why we are encouraged to keep the altar of our lives burning for God and to keep walking intentionally in all that we do.

And he died for all, that those who live should no longer live for themselves but for him who died for them and was raised again. (2 Corinthians 5:15)

We cannot be equally yoked together with unbelievers, as Christ has saved us by His death on the cross of Calvary. He who has no sin became the sin of the world and the sacrificial lamb. He paid the wages of the sin of the whole world.

Jesus Christ died for all, then all died, and we came alive through the resurrection power that brought Jesus Christ to life and gave us a new birth . As we were being conformed unto his death, we no longer live for ourselves but for Him who died for us and rose again. Hallelujah!

God has reconciled us to Himself through Jesus Christ, and old things have passed away . He has given us the ministry of reconciliation, as God was in Christ, reconciling the world to Himself. He made Him who knew no sin to be sin for us, that we might become the righteousness of God in Him.

14 Do not be yoked together with unbelievers. For what do righteousness and wickedness have in common? Or what fellow

ship can light have with darkness? 15 What harmony is there between Christ and Belial? Or what does a believer have in common with an unbeliever? 16 What agreement is there between the temple of God and idols? For we are the temple of the living God. As God has said: "I will live with them and walk among them, and I will be their God, and they will be my people." 17 Therefore, "Come out from them and be separate, says the Lord. Touch no unclean thing, and I will receive you." 18 And, "I will be a Father to you, and you will be my sons and daughters, says the Lord Almighty." (2 Corinthians 6:14-18)

Being unequally yoked will frustrate your walk with Christ in holiness, having fellowship with unfruitful workers of darkness. It will be out of order, as you will not have the kind of life that God desires for you because darkness will always be a drawback to a believer. Stand fast, therefore, in the liberty wherewith Christ hath made us free, and be not entangled again with the yoke of bondage

It is for freedom that Christ has set us free. Stand firm, then, and do not let yourselves be burdened again by a yoke of slavery. (Galatians 5:1).

As believers and children of the Highest, we are admonished to flee from every appearance of evil. The sin of sexual immorality is a sin against one's body, whereas every other sin is committed outside the body. Our body is not for sexual immorality but for the Lord. Sexual sin is a very serious matter, as the Bible warns that anyone who engages in it and defiles the temple of God , him shall God destroy. The unrighteous will not inherit the kingdom of God . Sexual sin defiles us —it's a no-go area, as it is sinful to have sex outside marriage . Let the marriage bed be undefiled, for God will judge the sexually immoral and adulterous.

Marriage should be honored by all, and the marriage bed kept pure, for God will judge the adulterer and all the sexually immoral. (Hebrews 13:4).

Sex should be used the way He commanded it —in a holy matrimonial bed. God does not take the sin of sexual immorality lightly, as it is degrading: "Every other sin a person commits is outside the body, but a sexually immoral person sins against his own body ." We are united in Christ in Spirit because He is our source, so there is no justification in joining our body with a harlot or anything else outside marriage.

If anyone destroys God's temple, God will destroy that person; for God's temple is sacred, and you together are that temple. (1 Corinthians 3:17)

This sin has destroyed lives, people, destinies, and marriages and has brought untimely death rather than building people up to excel. It's a no-go area, as its consequences unleash more grief than the pleasure it portrays. It's a great deception, as there is no form of sexual sin that should be neglected, as they all defile our bodies. Sex should be used the way God commanded it — between married couples. We should stay away from pornographic pictures or watching them so as not to be tempted beyond measure . All

sexual perversions — masturbation, bestiality, homosexuality, lesbianism, premature sexual relationships, extramarital affairs, and undue closeness with the opposite sex — have led many into temptation. A lot have ended up with what they did not bargain for.

May God give you the grace to resist the temptation of being tempted beyond your control and to say no to the sin of sexual immorality of any kind, in Jesus' name. Amen.

3 But among you there must not be even a hint of sexual immorality, or of any kind of impurity, or of greed, because these are improper for God's holy people. 4 Nor should there be obscenity, foolish talk or coarse joking, which are out of place, but rather thanksgiving. 5 For of this you can be sure: No immoral, impure or greedy person — such a person is an idolater — has any inheritance

in the kingdom of Christ and of God. (Ephesians 5:3-5)

Repentance

Everyone has a history. God brought Abraham out of a pagan family and the Israelites out of slavery in Egypt. He is today calling you out from living a sinful life and to embrace the truth. Repentance comes with urgency — do not delay any further so as to enjoy the good of the land and eternal life in Jesus Christ.

"There is basically no fun and reward in a life of sin as it breeds only guilt, death, and eternal anguish." - Alice Kalu.

Repentance is the bedrock of Christian life; it is one of the sure ways of ensuring our eternity.

Repentance is the activity of reviewing one's actions and feeling contrite or regretful for past wrongs, which is accompanied by a commitment to actual actions that show and prove a change for the better.

Contrition is a state of feeling remorseful and penitent, with a sense of guilt and a desire for the atonement of your sins staring right at you. You become broken-hearted with grief for having offended God. You feel crushed in spirit and humbled. The good news is that, at this point, God is closer to you than you can ever imagine. You are not alone, as this marks the turning point in your life in identifying who you are and realising the son or daughter of whom you are. Repentance brings about a change for the better. It is an overhaul of a bad character, making a commitment to personal change to live a more responsible human life.

"If we confess our sins, he is faithful and just to forgive us our sins, and to cleanse us from all unrighteousness." (1 John 1:9)

It is only in a place of true repentance that the altar of your life can be set on fire through prayer. It is the platform upon which every other promise of God thrives.

"As a born-again Christian, you become pliable in the hand of God. He will break and remould you for new things to be grafted into your life. This is because God does not use a filthy vessel.

Repentance gives us access to the secret things of God, and then we start living a life of dominion.

Repentance helps us tap into the joy of our union with Christ in order to weaken the urge to do anything contrary to God's will. It strengthens our relationship with God. We feel whole and brand new as the Holy Spirit begins to work out reconciliation between

God and man. Our relationship is restored with Him as He offers us new opportunities and charts a new course for our lives.

Life without Christ is filled with crises, just like the Israelites, who at one point were not receiving God's blessing and help and were taken into captivity for years in Babylon. The Lord is not lacking in the ability to save at all, but their sins created a barrier between them and God. The same is the case with us today.

The power of repentance opens your eyes to see how much you have wronged God. You admit your sins, and in your place of prayer, you ask for forgiveness . You will realise that sin is equal to death, and you will hate it with perfect hatred, knowing how destructive it is as it hinders one from fulfilling their destiny. The god of this world can no longer hold you as a prisoner with all the lies he has fed your mind with.

God's words become a mirror through which you see yourself. And with that, you come to the realisation that you cannot do anything by yourself except through Christ, who strengthens you.

Through repentance, the promises of God and the mission of Jesus Christ on earth are being enjoyed by genuine born-again Christians. His agenda is to save us, heal us, and deliver us. In like manner, we will also know the devil for who he is —to kill, steal, and destroy. And then we will know better.

"What shall it profit a man, if he shall gain the whole world, and lose his own soul?" (Mark 8:36)

So, repentance brings you to a place where you start seeking eternal things. As you seek eternal things, the supernatural power of God in you will start revealing itself , helping you to live a victorious life.

Today, if you hear the voice of the Lord, do not harden your heart. There is no condemnation for those who are in Christ Jesus. Through repentance, we are able to reconcile and walk together with Christ.

"Do not turn your back on God, because one day you will meet Him face to face, and it might be too late." (My quote)

Turn around and seek Jesus Christ before it is too late. When you receive Him as your Lord and personal Saviour, He gives you the power to do all things —even what you think is impossible — because there is no impossibility with God. You need such power in the days that we live in now.

Prayer of Repentance

Oh God, I confess you as my Lord and personal Saviour. Thank you for sending Jesus Christ, your only begotten Son, to die for me on the cross of Calvary in order to set me free from captivity and eternal damnation. I am so sorry for my evil deeds. I plead the blood of Jesus, and I genuinely repent of all my sins. Forgive me all my sins and cleanse me with the blood of Jesus. In Jesus' name, I pray, Amen.

Believe this prayer you have just said, and start a new walk of faith.

Brokenness

It is a cardinal point for a Christian to make heaven. Through brokenness, the fruit of the Holy Spirit is made manifest in the life of a believer.

But the fruit of the Spirit is love, joy, peace, forbearance, kind ness, goodness, faithfulness, gentleness and self-control. Against such things there is no law. (Galatians 5:22-23)

A man begins to exhibit the behaviour of one who is filled with the Holy Spirit as he brings forth fruit, which is vital for revival to take place in his life. Absolute surrender, willingness to fulfil God's purpose, calling, and desire ; submitting to God's authority ; yielding yourself to the will of God ; dying to the worldly system ; the love of Christ growing in you, making you pliable in God's hand by doing His will , even if others misunderstand you.

You don't complain when others are preferred before you when your suggestion is not taken ; you are ready to make restitution; you remain calm in the face of provocation; you let God have His way; you are completely emptied of oneself, completely emptied of pride; you are completely slain on the altar of God; you are of one mind with God; you hate what God hates and love what God loves; you are conformed to the image of God; you have the ability to tame the soul and your emotions. A broken person thinks before he speaks , not the other way around.

To live a crucified life means inner transformation, being quick to repent and take correction, honouring and appreciating others, instant obedience to God, self-control under crises or pressure, and humbling and honouring God no matter the height of life that you have attained.

It was pride that destroyed the devil, as he wanted to make himself a match for God. Don't allow the subtle nature of the devil to rob you of your salvation, as he has used this instrument of pride to cause firebrand Christians to backslide . That is why God wants us to be broken and humble, as that will keep us focused and in check in our kingdom race. Do not allow the devil to deceive you or make you think highly of yourself. He has nothing to offer. What he has to offer is counterfeit, and his strategy is deception, lies, and seduction of the simple -minded.

12 How you have fallen from heaven, morning star, son of the dawn! You have been cast down to the earth, you who once laid low the nations! 13 You said in your heart, "I will ascend to the heavens; I will raise my throne above the stars of God; I will sit enthroned on the mount of assembly, on the utmost heights of Mount Zaphon. 14 I will ascend above the tops of the clouds; I will make myself like the Most High." 15 But you are brought down to the realm of the dead, to the depths of the pit. 16 Those who see you stare at you, they ponder your fate: "Is this the man who shook the earth and made kingdoms tremble, 17 the man who made the world a wilderness, who overthrew its cities and would not let his captives go home?" (Isaiah 14:12-17)

Nehemiah was born in exile, and he became the cupbearer of King Artaxerxes, the Persian king. During the reign of King Artaxerxes, in his year of captivity, the burden to rebuild the wall of Jerusalem came upon him when he heard it was in ruins. The king noticed that his countenance had changed and that he looked sad. So, the king enquired of him , "Why is your face sad since you are not sick ?" He told him about the condition of Jerusalem and the ruined city walls, as the people were being plundered and the city gates were burned with fire , with no wall of protection around his people. He made his plea known to the king that if it pleased him, he should grant him permission to go back to Jerusalem and rebuild the city wall. The king was pleased to grant his request and also made provisions for the rebuilding, writing a letter regarding the matter. The king gave him all the necessary support because the hand of the Lord was upon him.

In rebuilding the city wall, he faced many challenges from his opposition —Sanballat, Tobiah, and Geshem—as they were filled with envy towards him. These men tried to frustrate them and mocked Nehemiah's vision. But because the Lord was on his side, he continued to grow stronger, making great progress in rebuilding the ruined city of Jerusalem. When these men saw his zeal and progress in reconstructing the city wall, they sent a message inviting him to a meeting in order to harm him : "Come, let us meet together among the villages in the plain of Ono." But their intention was evil.

Because the Spirit of God was upon him, and he had the gift of discernment, knowing that they did not mean well for him, he refused to go to them. They wanted him to come down to them , but he said , "I am doing great work, so I cannot come down ."That is brokenness. Many people without this attribute have gone to dine with their enemies with their eyes open, knowing fully well the danger but thinking in their minds that they can handle it or outsmart them.

TO PROVE TO THEM THAT THEY KNOW WHAT THEY ARE DOING. SOMETIMES, KNOW WHEN TO IGNORE AND TIME SHALL TELL.

Some have come down from where God placed them, straight into the hands of their enemies and even into their graves. God, have mercy on us in Jesus' name. The Bible says that we should resist the devil, and he will flee from us.

Submit yourselves, then, to God. Resist the devil, and he will flee from you. (James 4:7)

¹When word came to Sanballat, Tobiah, Geshem the Arab and the rest of our enemies that I had rebuilt the wall and not a gap was left in it-though up to that time I had not set the doors in the gates ² Sanballat and Geshem sent me this message: "Come, let us meet together in one of the villages on the plain of Ono." But they were scheming to harm me; ³ so I sent messengers to them with this reply: "I am carrying on a great project and cannot go down. Why should the work stop while I leave it and go down to you?" 4 Four times they sent me the same message, and each time I gave them the same answer. ⁵ Then, the fifth time, Sanballat sent his aide to me with the same message, and in his hand was an unsealed letter 6 in which was written: "It is reported among the nations-and Geshem says it is true-that you and the Jews are plotting to revolt, and therefore you are building the wall. Moreover, according to these reports you are about to become their king ⁷ and have even appointed prophets to make this proclamation about you in Jerusalem: 'There is a king in Judah!' Now this report will get back to the king; so come, let us meet together." ⁸ I sent him this reply: "Nothing like what you are saying is happening; you are just making it up out of your head." ⁹ They were all trying to frighten us, thinking, "Their hands will get too weak for the work, and it will not be completed." But I prayed, "Now strengthen my

hands." (Nehemiah 6:1–9)

Jesus Christ, our role model, also demonstrated this attribute when He was mocked by the people to come down from the cross. They said He claimed He would destroy the temple and rebuild it in three days. He spoke in parables, and they did not understand that the temple He was referring to was not the physical temple that took them 47 years to build but His own body. His death gave birth to the Church of Christ and to our bodies becoming temples of God through the Holy Spirit, who sustains us. They said He saved others but could not save Himself. But Jesus' mission on the cross was not for Himself but for all. Jesus did not despise the cross or refuse to die in such a manner, as His purpose was to save the world. He refused to come down not because He lacked the power but because He had a mission to fulfil. He was broken and completely slain on the altar of God. He did not need to prove anything to them , nor did He equate Himself with God to abort His mission to die for mankind and save us from eternal condemnation.

Brokenness is when you have the power to take action or react, which may be influenced by external factors or pressure, but in- stead, you control your emotions by dying to self, submitting to

God's authority, and not being intoxicated by the power you possess, but applying wise judgment to your actions through the help of the Holy Spirit, who grants discernment. (My definition or quote)

SEEK A SPIRIT-FILLED CHURCH OF CHRIST

Seek a Spirit-filled church of Christ, and don't go seeking God in a dead place, as we have many unholy, dead, and polluted altars where the Spirit of God does not dwell . Seek God on a living altar and not a dead altar that lacks fire. True worshippers seek God in a living altar and keep their bodies sacred. They earnestly seek God and take deeper steps with Him , as the secret of the Lord is with those who love Him, as He has demonstrated to our forefathers. There is a need for you to grow in holiness and treat your body as sacred. When you grow in holiness, you will be able to discern an unholy altar, as you are also a spiritual temple of God. Our body is the dwelling place of the Holy Spirit. But if you fail to take this into cognisance, you will continue to be a babe Christian who cannot do much in kingdom service, as you will keep feeding on milk and not meat. Such Christians, most times, become vulnerable to shepherds who call themselves and are taken advantage of.

It is not every door that is opened as a church that you must enter. That is why, as a child of God, you should go the extra mile to seek Him intentionally because, by doing so, you will receive the spirit of discernment . He cannot show you many things at once because you might not have the understanding and capacity to manage divine information. But walking with Him every day takes you deeper into His divine presence and makes you more knowledgeable in spiritual matters.

There is depth, and there is depth indeed, in Christendom. The knowledge you have about God determines the countless victories in your life as a believer. Believers will stand firm even in the face of adversity, knowing that it will produce strength and faith. When the sea rages with billows of waves, believers will pray and patiently allow the fullness of God Almighty to fill their deep des

pairing situation.

A deep need calls for a deep panacea, as deep calleth unto deep (Psalm 42:7).

To Live a Holy Life

And a highway will be there; it will be called the Way of Holiness; it will be for those who walk on that Way. The unclean will not journey on it; wicked fools will not go about on it. (Isaiah 35:8)

We need to follow the highway of holiness for the temple within us to keep burning. Without holiness, we cannot see God. Through the blood of the Lamb, we enter into the Holy of Holies. His righteousness is imputed to us, qualifying us to stand in His presence. The highway is a way of victory. Jesus is the only way to our salvation. There is no other way to get to the Father except through Him. **NO OTHER WAY!**

Deep calls to deep in the roar of your waterfalls; all your waves and breakers have swept over me. (1 Corinthians 6:9-10)

The people mentioned in 1 Corinthians 6:9-10 — the unclean — cannot live a holy life because they are so engrossed in the flesh. The flesh does not understand the things of the Spirit. They are two different things and irreconcilable. When you engage in spiritual exercises and walk in obedience to the Word of God, He will reveal deep and secret things to you that others cannot see. You become a phenomenon , seeing beyond physical sight and understanding heavenly languages and signals. The spiritual and physical worlds are two different things. There is a vast difference, and that is why, as a child of God, we are to use the spiritual realm to address the physical by calling forth those things that are not as though they were

(Romans 4:17). You have the power to effect changes from the spiritual realm into the physical realm. That is the style of our Father in Heaven, and we must manifest His character.

Without fellowship with Him, you will go astray and get lost in this world. Christians are meant to **live** on the highway of life. The highway of life is a path and direction to follow through the help of the Holy Spirit. It is not the way of sinners. It is a lifestyle that launches Christians into a supernatural and victorious life that has been predestined for them. It is a life that leads to holiness and obedience to the Word of God and helps us to soar like the eagle that we are. This kind of life activates the giant in us and helps us to be spiritually minded rather than carnally minded, which leads to enmity with Christ.

13 "Enter through the narrow gate. For wide is the gate and broad is the road that leads to destruction, and many enter through it. 14 But small is the gate and narrow the road that leads to life, and only a few find it. Matthew 7:13-14

We were admonished to follow the narrow road, for broad is the way that leads to death. But most Christians do not adhere to this instruction , yet they want a change in their situation. The kingdom of God has principles — **precept upon precept and line upon line.**

We are meant to walk circumspectly, not as fools. We cannot drink from the L's cup and also from the cup of the devil. We are either cold or hot ; we cannot be both. We want God's blessings, but we don't want to follow the path of righteousness. We want to go through the wide, broad way so as to carry all our excess baggage and walk in the flesh.

Apostle Paul admonishes Timothy to endure hardship as a soldier of Christ. The strait road is not for lazy Christians but for mature Christians who have graduated from suckling milk to eating solid food.

I gave you milk, not solid food, for you were not yet ready for it. Indeed, you are still not ready. (1 Corinthians 3:2)

Holiness is within and without. It starts from inside a man and is seen outside as the light of God in a man. It) is inside -out and not like the Pharisees and hypocrites who glittered on the outside and appeared holy but, on the inside, were full of greed and asked people to do things they themselves could not

do.

"Woe to you, teachers of the law and Pharisees, you hypocrites! You clean the outside of the cup and dish, but inside they

are full of greed and self-indulgence. (Matthew 23:25)

Man is a spirit who dwells in the body with the soul. Our spirit is made to connect with the Spirit of God , who brings all truth to us and helps us to live a fulfilled life — not just as mere men but as spiritual beings. But sin in man has made that impossible and disconnected him from the original plan of God. Man has lived a carnal life (a life in the flesh), powerless, as to be carnally minded is death even while living. This life has subjected man to live by intellectual knowledge and emotions rather than through the Spirit, which connects to God for superintelligence and revelation of full kingdom mysteries that help man live a supernatural life. The Spirit of God unleashes power on us, as He did not give us a spirit of fear but of **power, love, and a sound mind**.

As a child of God and a born -again believer, we are now born of God.

Children born not of natural descent, nor of human decision or a husband's will, but born of God. (John 1:13)

He has beckoned us to come to Him — all of us who are heavy laden — and He will give us rest, as His anointing shall break every yoke and lift every burden . This anointing comes to us through the

Holy Spirit, bringing ease into our lives. The Holy Spirit ignites the fire of God within us and sets the altar of God in our lives on fire. It is very important for a child of God to be imbued with the Holy Spirit. Without Him, we can do nothing. The world will toss us up and down as it makes way for those who know where they are going. The Holy Spirit is your compass and guide in life.

For a righteous believer indwelt by the Holy Spirit, **you will bear fruit and be productive.**

7 If you remain in me and my words remain in you, ask whatever you wish, and it will be done for you. 8 This is to my Father's glory, that you bear much fruit, showing yourselves to be my disciples.

9 "As the Father has loved me, so have I loved you. Now remain in my love. 10 If you keep my commands, you will remain in my love, just as I have kept my Father's commands and remain in his love. 11 I have told you this so that my joy may be in you and that your joy may be complete. 12 My command is this: Love each other as I have loved you. 13 Greater love has no one than this: to lay down one's life for one's friends. 14 You are my friends if you do what I command. 15 I no longer call you servants, because a servant

does not know his master's business. Instead, I have called you friends, for everything that I learned from my Father I have made known to you. [16] You did not choose me, but I chose you and appointed you so that you might go and bear fruit—fruit that will not choose me, but I chose you and appointed you so that you might go and bear fruit—fruit that will last—and so that whatever you ask in my name the Father will give you. (John 15:7-16)

FORGIVENESS OF OTHERS AND YOURSELF

Forgiveness is very vital in Christendom. For a Christian to strive successfully in the kingdom race, we need to be merciful in heart and relate others with a compassionate and forgiving spirit. Imagine the life of Stephen being brought to an abrupt end, and he still went ahead to pray for the evildoers. He let go of every spirit of heaviness, even in death.

In a typical life experience, some Christians do not let go of their hearts of bad experiences from those who offend them. We can draw some lessons from some of these life experiences and thank God that we live to tell the stories. Open up a new chapter in your life and walk circumspectly. Assuming you contributed to part of what you have just gone through by man's carnal nature, forgive yourself and free yourself from being judgemental.

55 But Stephen, full of the Holy Spirit, looked up to heaven and saw the glory of God, and Jesus standing at the right hand of God. 56 "Look," he said, "I see heaven open and the Son of Man standing at the right hand of God." (Acts 7:55–56)

Unforgiveness is toxic in our system, coupled with the pain inflicted on us by the offender. Today, some believers boast that they will never forget, let alone forgive. It is bitterness that does not leave us any better and is one of the weapons that the devil has used to send a lot of believers to an early grave. Medically, it has been associated with a lot of degenerative diseases, for example, cancer, high blood pressure, and eating disorders, which can occur as a result of unforgiveness. This can negatively impact your health condition. You add more pain to yourself when you fail to forgive. Forgiveness is for our own good.

As a believer, walk in obedience to the word of God and allow God to avenge for you. Jesus Christ taught us about forgiveness, to forgive **70× 7** in a day, which is highly impossible for someone to wrong you 490 times in a day. It is not even easy for you to keep counting how many times you have been offended by one person. In a nutshell, He is asking you not to keep offence in your mind so as not to lose yourself.

Jesus answered, "I tell you, not seven times, but seventy-seven times. (Matthew 18:22)

Imbibe the teaching and allow the Holy Spirit to divinely lead you in the process of forgiving those who have hurt you, as unforgiveness can also hamper the degree of the flame on our altar. Imbibe the teaching and allow the Holy Spirit to divinely lead you.

THE FEAR OF GOD GUIDE US INTO OBEDIENCE

The fear of God in a man is the beginning of wisdom. Humility and fear of the Lord bring riches, honour, and life. The fear of God is the foundation of Christendom. Without the fear of God, we really cannot serve Him.

Human life is short, but it is worth living in the fear of God, as it passes too quickly, like a flower. May we not spend our time on earth living in ignorance of who we are by making many errors. The light of God shall shine upon us, as Christ has translated us from the kingdom of darkness into His marvellous light to fellowship with Him.

Proclaiming, "The Lord is upright; he is my Rock, and there is no wickedness in him." (Psalm 92:15)

Put God first, and your life will be balanced. When we close our fellowship with God, a person's desires in his heart will not align with God's will and purpose for his life. His will and purpose for us are our calling and destiny — His plan for our lives.

As believers, we have to submit to God's authority and His ordinances. If we cannot do what He asks us to do, then there is no need to call Him Father. We should trust Him enough to walk in tune with His instructions. Our obedience to Him is better than sacrifice, as disobedience is costly, and sacrifice cannot take the place of obedience.

Consider the case of King Saul, who was commanded to destroy the Amalekites until they were completely consumed. He went to war and gained victory—not by his strength, but by God's grace. However, his victory came with a condition: to destroy everything. Yet, he failed to fulfil his part. We must obey God and not seek to please men, as Saul did when he sought to appease his soldiers by keeping some of the spoils and sparing King Agag of the Amalekites.

God wants us to have unwavering faith in Him because His word is not idle—it is a commandment that we must execute with reverence. There are things in our lives that spiritually represent a stronghold, and as believers, we need to utterly destroy them. If we do not, they have the power to keep us in perpetual bondage. (King Agag and some of the spoils represent things we must completely do away with, no matter how dignified they may appear.) Saul enjoyed the charade for a moment, but it was short-lived, as he placed his egotistical desires above God's commandment.

11 "I regret that I have made Saul king, because he has turned away from me and has not carried out my instructions." Samuel was angry, and he cried out to the Lord all that night.

12 Early in the morning Samuel got up and went to meet Saul, but he was told, "Saul has gone to Carmel. There he has set up a monument in his own honor and has turned and gone on down to Gilgal."

13 When Samuel reached him, Saul said, "The Lord bless you! I have carried out the Lord's instructions."

14 But Samuel said, "What then is this bleating of sheep in my ears? What is this lowing of cattle that I hear?"

15 Saul answered, "The soldiers brought them from the Amalekites; they spared the best of the sheep and cattle to sacrifice to the Lord your God, but we totally destroyed the rest."

16 "Enough!" Samuel said to Saul. "Let me tell you what the Lord said to me last night." "Tell me," Saul replied. 17 Samuel said, "Although you were once small in your own eyes, did you not become the head of the tribes of Israel? The Lord anointed you king over Israel. 18 And he sent you on a mission, saying, 'Go and completely destroy those wicked people, the Amalekites; wage war against them until you have wiped them out.' 19 Why did you not obey the Lord? Why did you pounce on the plunder and do evil in the eyes of the Lord?"

20 "But I did obey the Lord," Saul said. "I went on the mission the Lord assigned me. I completely destroyed the Amalekites and

brought back Agag their king. 21 The soldiers took sheep and cattle from the plunder, the best of what was devoted to God, in order to sacrifice them to the Lord your God at Gilgal."

22 But Samuel replied: "Does the Lord delight in burnt offerings and sacrifices as much as in obeying the Lord? To obey is better than sacrifice, and to heed is better than the fat of rams. (1 Samuel 15:11–22)

FAITH

Without faith, no man can please God.

"Now faith is the assurance of things hoped for, the conviction of things not seen." (Hebrews 11:1). Through faith, you believe and proclaim victory — that the situation will turn out for your good because you are a child of God. It is a strong belief that an individual places his whole trust in God and does not turn to the left or right. It is a high level of trust. In faith, we experience life-transforming and destiny-changing results, which God has already provided for us. God has given every one of us a measure of faith; all we need to do is develop it and intentionally increase our faith in trusting Him. Faith is very important for man, as it grants us access to what God has given to us from the beginning of creation. Faith appropriates God's supplies and promises to us. We need an optimistic mindset that will be commensurate with positive responses for results. Faith is not passive but active; you must act upon it, as faith without works is dead.

Without faith, no man can receive from, see, or please God. You are a child of God by faith. It was by faith that Abraham was counted as righteous. By the shield of faith, you extinguish all the flaming darts of the evil ones by believing.

23 "Truly I tell you, if anyone says to this mountain, 'Go, throw yourself into the sea,' and does not doubt in their heart but believes that what they say will happen, it will be done for them. 24 Therefore I tell you, whatever you ask for in prayer, believe that you have received it, and it will be yours. (Mark 11:23-24)

Faith pleases God more than anything else. God saved Abraham in every situation of his life because of his trust in Him. Your faith in Christ goes a long way in determining what you can receive from God, the kind of relationship that can exist between you and God, and how deep it can be. With faith in you, you will realise that there is nothing beyond, above, over, or beneath that God cannot do. He made all things, and He is sovereign—there is nothing impossible for Him. By human strength shall no man prevail, but through faith in God, we can do all things.

Let him who asks from God ask without wavering. I pray for you, the reader of this book, that God will increase your faith and help it to be strong and unwavering so that you may receive and not become like a rolling stone that gathers no moss.

6 But when you ask, you must believe and not doubt, because the one who doubts is like a wave of the sea, blown and tossed by the wind. 7 That person should not expect to receive anything from the Lord. (James 1:6-7)

The scribes kept asking for signs to convince them because their hearts were so hardened. The power of God lies in His word. We are not supposed to be seekers of signs but fire-branded believers who will call forth things from the spiritual realm, just as Jesus Christ did.

They still did not believe that he had been blind and had received his sight until they sent for the man's parents. (John 9:18)

Guard Your Heart

"Above all else, guard your heart, for everything you do flows from it." (Proverbs 4:23)

As a man thinketh, so he is. Our heart is the source of everything that we do. As we think in our hearts, that becomes the reflection of our outward appearance. It is the source of everything else in your life and your posture in life because from it flows the issues of life. Your mind is like a garden that gives a true reflection of the seeds you have planted, manifesting in your physical appearance. Your mind overflows into your thoughts, words, actions, and ultimately what you become. In other words, your life is a reflection of your thoughts. If your mind is toxic, you will become poisonous and unhealthy to yourself and everyone around you. We position our lives and win the battles of life right in our minds.

Make it your top priority to plant the living word of God in your mind. Feed yourself with the word of God, meditate on it, speak it often, and do not be swayed by negative emotions.

It is very important that we guard our hearts. To guard the heart is to diligently protect it both in the natural realm — by being conscious of our thoughts — and in the spiritual realm through the word of God. A formula has been given in the Bible to help us understand what is going on in our hearts and to protect them.

"Finally, brothers and sisters, whatever is true, whatever is noble, whatever is right, whatever is pure, whatever is lovely, whatever is admirable — if anything is excellent or praiseworthy — think about such things." (Philippians 4:8)

Be careful what you allow into your mind. If the outcome is not what you want, do not grant access to it. The result you get cannot be different from what you have imprinted in your mind. Most battles we win physically are, most of the time, won first in our minds.

STUDYING THE WORD OF GOD AND INTERNALISING IT

Find time to read the Bible, memorise and learn the scriptures. Allow the Holy Spirit to help you to change through praying and fasting as you intentionally and decisively change your attitude and your old ways of life. We need to depend on God, not on our own cleverness or man-made solutions. Through fasting, you enter into the spiritual realm, where more revelation and illumination of the word of God will become more glaring to you and help you to prepare for the task ahead of you.

Take conscious steps to correct all your wrong decisions, pursue the things of God with passion, and do not grieve the Holy Spirit. Spend quality time with people who will help you grow in your new faith in Christ — genuine born-again Christians who have the fire of God in them. Allow your heart to be tender and filled with the love of Christ — the heart of flesh and not of stone. To love in such a way that one will feel like he has seen the face of God. Like Jacob said to Esau after many years of being estranged from Esau after stealing his birthright, and how he was received and forgiven by his brother

Esau. He felt he had seen the face of God; he must have felt an overwhelming love and genuine forgiveness from his brother that made him feel that way. We need to demonstrate the love of God and impart it in a likewise manner.

"No, please!" said Jacob. "If I have found favor in your eyes, accept this gift from me. For to see your face is like seeing the face of God, now that you have received me favorably. (Genesis 33:10)

We really do not have an excuse not to exhibit and be the epitome of love. For God so loved the world that He gave His only begotten Son to die for the world. You should love without condition and reservation. Be selfless, filled with agape love, and demonstrate sacrificial concern for one another. Let all that we do be done in love. Love is giving. It has to cost you something. It is not passive. Yours could be forgiveness, preaching the gospel with an iota of love and not condemning people, remembering where God found you, etc. For as we walk in this divine direction and instruction, we will continue to transform to God's glory, to the knowledge that all things have been given to us, AND THAT THE TEMPLE IS IN YOU. Holiness within and without is not negotiable, and the words of Apostle Paul, inspired by the Holy Spirit, will become our confession.

"Whether Paul or Apollos or Cephas or the world or life or death or the present or the future—all are yours." (1 Corinthians 3:22)

CONSEQUENCES OF NOT KNOWING WHO YOU ARE IN THE INDULGENCE OF THE SIN OF SEXUAL IMMORALITY

Sexual intercourse has become common in the world that we live in today. It is no longer sacred. Unlike other kinds of sins, sexual immorality has a peculiarity as a sin against one's body. It crushes the spirit, wounds the soul, and exposes one to all manners of dangers. There is nothing exciting about it, especially when you weigh the cons. It is risky and more dangerous than you can imagine. It opens the door for other kinds of afflictions in the lives of men, such as sexually transmitted diseases, depression, guilt, emotional and psychological unrest, and, finally, death and damnation. Apart from spiritual death, it sometimes leads to the physical death of the victims. There is no need to hide the sin of sexual immorality in the dark because, at the right time, it will find you out. The devil is raging and destroying lives through this particular sin. A shop attendant resigned from her place of work because her one-night stand was equivalent to her monthly salary, and she made it a headline without any feeling of ignominy. She did not think of the long-run risk involved and the spiritual aspect of defiling her body as a spiritual being. Rather, she took pride in it. Things are not always what they seem to be. All that glitters is not gold. The world flaunts sexual immorality with dignity.

Teen pregnancy is on the increase as a result of the sexual looseness of teenagers, which has resulted in death for some while carrying out abortion. Sometimes, teenagers play it as a game to show sexual prowess and how many rounds each can go. Unfortunately, some did not live to know who won. Some made videos of the act to blackmail and display for all to see when their terms were not met. Some practise bestiality. Some have fallen victim to sex traffickers, leaving their loved ones in grief, not knowing their whereabouts. Some have lost their positions and reputations through this act; many marriages have hit the rocks because of infidelity. Even some ministers of God are not spared, just as David fell for it by watching live pornography that led him to commit adultery, which attracted a curse upon his household.

It has become a norm that even many commercial adverts depict symbols of sex for matters that are not even related to the subject. Many lives have been damaged beyond repair; some have contracted diseases and infections that they will have to live with throughout their lifetime. A lot of people are having infertility problems because of their past lives. Siblings are having sex; incest is on the increase. It was in the news about a mother who was having sex with her own son, to the point that she wanted a wholesale of the bounty and decided that they should tie the knot — and they wedded. Some fathers are sleeping with their daughters and interfering in their relationships so as not to be with someone else. A lot of damage and mishaps have happened to young and old people in the supposed pleasure of sex.

In all of this, who is the loser? The culprit (the devil) walks away as if nothing happened, without any concern, but alas, the man suffers. All this is just a few moments of pleasure that may not last a whole day but could lead to living a lifetime of regret, pain, anguish, and, sometimes, committing suicide — except a miracle happens.

Some Biblical illustrations of the consequences of the sin of sexual immorality.

A lot of life has been cut short and wasted by the enemy, and some people have been kept busy in a field that is in no way related to what God has called them to be. That you are busy doing something does not mean you are in the area of your divine calling.

A lot of people have died before their time, not fulfilling their calling and destiny, because of the sin of fornication and adultery.

This is clearly illustrated in the story of Samson. He was spiritually ordained from the womb as a prophet, a Nazirite, to serve God and deliver his people from their enemies.

Intermarriage with a Philistine woman was a no-go area for Samson. He was a Nazirite. Gaza was the furthest city of the Philistines from Sam's home, which symbolises how far Samson always went away from God's presence to sleep with a woman in Gaza. Women were his problem, and this weakness finally led to his death.

He broke all the Nazirite vows attached to his calling. He was not supposed to drink wine, but he hosted a drinking party. He touched the carcass of a lion, which he was not supposed to touch, as Nazirites were forbidden from contact with dead things. Samson always sought the Lord's deliverance, but as soon as he was over with it, he went back to his old ways.

His uncut hair was the only Nazirite vow left unhampered, and this shows how lightly he took it when he finally revealed it to Delilah. And his power was gone. The sin of the lust of the eyes and sexual immorality destroyed him. Finally, he was captured by his enemies, his eyes were plucked out, and they channelled his strength into the wrong services, using him as a human machine to grind their grains and for entertainment. They mocked him in the midst of his hopeless situation, seeing that he had been captured and tamed by their wickedness.

This is still happening to some of the children of God, being used and destroyed by their enemies.

Many are grinding the grains and entertaining their enemies. Many men of valour have ended up serving those who ought to serve them. It is quite a pathetic situation when the prince becomes the servant.

"I have seen slaves on horseback, while princes go on foot like slaves." Ecclesiastes 10:7

When someone fails to know who they are, the enemy will use them to destroy themselves and others. The person's destiny and life will be wasted, just like what happened to Samson and the prince who became a servant. They lost their rightful places.

Prayer

Take this prayer:

- My body will not become an instrument of destruction to my life, in Jesus name, Amen.

- I refuse to be wasted by my enemies, in Jesus' name.

- My body will not yield to sexual looseness, in Je' mighty name, Amen.

Sexual immorality has done more havoc than we can ever imagine, as it has turned some princes and princesses into slaves in the camps of their enemies. Samson was supposed to deliver his people from the hands of their enemies, the Philistines, who always came and plundered them. But he failed and fell into their evil-crafted plans, which choked up his destiny and took his life with it — all because of his sexual looseness. Although he prayed to God for one last moment of victory over his enemies, and God heard him and granted his request, he could have done more and lived longer, but the enemy cut his life short.

"Again the Israelites did evil in the eyes of the Lord, so the Lord delivered them into the hands of the Philistines for forty years. [2] A certain man of Zorah, named Manoah, from the clan of the Danites, had a wife who was childless, unable to give birth. [3] The angel of the Lord appeared to her and said, "You are barren and childless, but you are going to become pregnant and give birth to a son. [4] Now see to it that you drink no wine or other fermented drink and that you do not eat anything unclean. [5] You will become pregnant and have a son whose head is never to be touched by a

razor because the boy is to be a Nazirite, dedicated to God from the womb. He will take the lead in delivering Israel from the hands of the Philistines." (Judges 13:1-5)

The Levite's Concubine

A Levite and his concubine were seeking shelter in a city where they could spend the night. They came across an old man who gave them a place to stay. While they were having some merriment to relax in the newly found apartment, some perverted men of the sons of Belial in Gibeah came to the man's house and requested sex with his guest. Since they could not have the Levite, they brought out his concubine and had sex with her until the breaking of dawn, and she died.

22 While they were enjoying themselves, some of the wicked men of the city surrounded the house. Pounding on the door, they shouted to the old man who owned the house, "Bring out the man who came to your house so we can have sex with him."

23 The owner of the house went outside and said to them, "No, my friends, don't be so vile. Since this man is my guest, don't do this outrageous thing. 24 Look, here is my virgin daughter, and his concubine. I will bring them out to you now, and you can use them and do to them whatever you wish. But as for this man, don't do such an outrageous thing."

25 But the men would not listen to him. So the man took his concubine and sent her outside to them, and they raped her and abused her throughout the night, and at dawn they let her go. 26 At daybreak the woman went back to the house where her master was staying, fell down at the door and lay there until daylight.

27 When her master got up in the morning and opened the door of the house and stepped out to continue on his way, there lay his concubine, fallen in the doorway of the house, with her hands on the threshold. 28 He said to her, "Get up; let's go." But there was no answer. Then the man put her on his donkey and set out for home. 29 When he reached home, he took a knife and cut up his concubine, limb by limb, into twelve parts and sent them into all the areas of Israel. 30 Everyone who saw it was saying to one another, "Such a thing has never been seen or done, not since the day the Israelites came up out of Egypt. Just imagine! We must do something! So speak up!" (Judges 19:22-30)

The Levites presented the matter to the assembly of the Israelites, and they summoned the Benjamites to release the men of Belial to them. But they were more interested in tribal solidarity than national interest and ignored the evil that these men had done. This act of sexual looseness and perversion almost wiped out the entire tribe of Gibeah, as the Israelites took united action against them. There was a war between the Benjamites and the Israelites, which nearly caused the extinction of the Benjamite tribe because they refused to release the children of Belial to the Israelites for appropriate punishment. The Benjamites were defeated in the war, and most of their mighty men of valour were killed, apart from the 600 men who escaped into the wilderness.

Just like a bird that flies into the bait of the hunter even when the trap is set before it, so do people keep falling into this evil web of sexual immorality, which comes with destruction.

King David (The man after God's own heart)

David killed a man, Uriah, one of his armies, with the sword of his enemies in order to cover his sin of adultery with Uriah's wife. David's intention was not to become a murderer, but in order to cover the sin of adultery that he committed in secret, which led to Bathsheba' conception for him, he masterminded a plan to kill Uriah, husband, who was one of his soldiers but was at the battlefield. He succeeded in killing him, but God was not happy with his dastardly act. And that single act alone brought misery and a curse into the life of David. God sent a prophet to deliver a message to him, as his act was not hidden before God: **"That the sword will not depart from his house"** (2 Sam 12:10). The prophecy came to pass as David's house was beset with internal strife amongst his children — death, violence, rancour… He was haunted by this sin even into his old age.

Sin has a way of punishing others as it affects them besides the person who has committed the sin. It can cause others to grieve. This sin alone almost destroyed the house of David and his throne as King of Israel. One of his sons, Amnon, had carnal knowledge of his stepsister, Tamar, and after the act, the stepsister he lusted after as if his next breath depended on her became disgusting and despicable in his sight. And when Absalom, Tamar's brother, became aware of what Amnon did to his sister, he sought revenge. After two years of waiting, the day finally came, as he never forgave his stepbrother Amnon, even when King David, their father, had tried to make peace between them.

Absalom beguilingly invited his brothers to his sheepshearers with approval from his father, a period when shepherds demonstrated their love for their sheep — a joyous festival. Before the invitation, he had already masterminded with his servant to kill Amnon among his other guests as the ceremony was going on. By his commandment, his servant killed Amnon, his stepbrother, and he fled from his father's presence. By the time he came back to Israel, Absalom and Da's relationship never remained the same.

The cordial relationship between him and his father was no longer there, as he became a rival to his father, to the point of seeking his father's life. He had sex with his father's concubines on the rooftop while his father was still alive. He sought to kill him, as he wanted to usurp his throne and become king by all means. He was supported even by some close associates and allies of his father, King David.

All these ugly incidents came to bear because of Da's grievous sin of adultery with Bathsheba, which did not just stop there. From an adulterer, he became a murderer. This is not for us to judge anyone in the Bible but for us to learn and not to fall into the same temptation. At the end of the day, Absalom died in a very pathetic way without a chance to defend himself. All this was rooted in the sin of King David.

"In the spring, at the time when kings go off to war, David sent Joab out with the king's men and the whole Israelite army. They destroyed the Ammonites and besieged Rabbah. But David remained in Jerusalem.

2 One evening David got up from his bed and walked around on the roof of the palace. From the roof he saw a woman bathing. The woman was very beautiful, 3 and David sent someone to find out about her. The man said, "She is Bathsheba, the daughter of

Eliam and the wife of Uriah the Hittite." 4 Then David sent messengers to get her. She came to him, and he slept with her. (Now she was purifying herself from her monthly uncleanness.) Then she went back home. 5 The woman conceived and sent word to David, saying, "I am pregnant."

6 So David sent this word to Joab: "Send me Uriah the Hittite." And Joab sent him to David. 7 When Uriah came to him, David asked him how Joab was, how the soldiers were and how the war was going. 8 Then David said to Uriah, "Go down to your house and wash your feet." So Uriah left the palace, and a gift from the king was sent after him. 9 But Uriah slept at the entrance to the palace with all his master's servants and did not go down to his house.

10 David was told, "Uriah did not go home." So he asked Uriah, "Haven't you just come from a military campaign? Why didn't you go home?"

11 Uriah said to David, "The ark and Israel and Judah are staying in tents,[a] and my commander Joab and my lord's men are camped in the open country. How could I go to my house to eat and drink and make love to my wife? As surely as you live, I will not do such a thing!"

12 Then David said to him, "Stay here one more day, and tomorrow I will send you back." So Uriah remained in Jerusalem that day and the next. 13 At David's invitation, he ate and drank with him, and David made him drunk. But in the evening Uriah went out to sleep on his mat among his master's servants; he did not go home.

14 In the morning David wrote a letter to Joab and sent it with Uriah. 15 In it he wrote, "Put Uriah out in front where the fighting is fiercest. Then withdraw from him so he will be struck down and die."

16 So while Joab had the city under siege, he put Uriah at a place where he knew the strongest defenders were. 17 When the men of the city came out and fought against Joab, some of the men in David's army fell; moreover, Uriah the Hittite died.

18 Joab sent David a full account of the battle. 19 He instructed the messenger: "When you have finished giving the king this account of the battle, 20 the king's anger may flare up, and he may ask you, 'Why did you get so close to the city to fight? Didn't you know they would shoot arrows from the wall? 21 Who killed Abimelek son of Jerub-Besheth[b]? Didn't a woman drop an upper millstone on him from the wall, so that he died in Thebez? Why

did you get so close to the wall?' If he asks you this, then say to him, 'Moreover, your servant Uriah the Hittite is dead.'"

22 The messenger set out, and when he arrived he told David everything Joab had sent him to say. 23 The messenger said to David, "The men overpowered us and came out against us in the open, but we drove them back to the entrance of the city gate. 24 Then the archers shot arrows at your servants from the wall, and some of the king's men died. Moreover, your servant Uriah the Hittite is dead."

25 David told the messenger, "Say this to Joab: 'Don't let this upset you; the sword devours one as well as another. Press the attack against the city and destroy it.' Say this to encourage Joab."

26 When Uriah's wife heard that her husband was dead, she mourned for him. 27 After the time of mourning was over, David had her brought to his house, and she became his wife and bore him a son. But the thing David had done displeased the Lord. (2 Samuel 11:1-27)

The Men of Gomorrah

The men of the city of Gomorrah wanted to have carnal knowledge of 's guests, the angels that visited him. They persisted to the point that they wanted to bring down the roof of Lot's house. Lot, knowing who his guests were and trying to protect them, offered his own daughters to them, but they refused. They did not even need a lot of protection. They were angels and not mere men. The Angel of the Lord struck them with spiritual blindness.

A lot of people have had sex with demonic, strange beings and have been struck with all kinds of afflictions and diseases.

Some people are spiritually blind; they see but cannot understand, as the enemy has emptied their virtue through the sin of sexual intercourse with them. Life is spiritual. You really have to pray to God to open your spiritual eye of understanding to help you see beyond the mere physical.

Benefits of Living the Kingdom Way

The benefits of living the kingdom way are uncountable, just like the air we breathe. Blessing and a prosperous life come from God, not through false prophets or false gods. You will enjoy a restoration of an Eden-like condition, and the peace of God that surpasses all human understanding will come to you as you live the kingdom way. You will have peace that surpasses all human understanding. The peace of God is inestimable. Nothing on earth can give you that peace besides God—not even the money that many people idolise and strive for by all means.

The Spirit of God will dwell in you, as He said in His word that when we abide in Him, He will also abide in us.

"4 Remain in me, as I also remain in you. No branch can bear fruit by itself; it must remain in the vine. Neither can you bear fruit unless you remain in me. 5 "I am the vine; you are the branches. If you remain in me and I in you, you will bear much fruit; apart from me you can do nothing. 6 If you do not remain in me, you are like a branch that is thrown away and withers; such branches are picked up, thrown into the fire and burned. 7 If you remain in me and my words remain in you, ask whatever you wish, and it will be done for you." (John 15:4-7)

A lot of men have carried out various spiritual exercises just to hear from God. When you live the kingdom way and walk in obedience to God's divine instruction, the Spirit of God will come to you naturally and effortlessly, as He has said: if we draw nearer to Him, He will also draw nearer to us. We are commanded to seek Him with all our strength and heart—not like the Pharisees, who seek Him not from their heart but as a matter of lip service, as they put on an outward appearance of holiness. Holiness is within and without, from the inside of a man, and is seen outside as the light of God in a man. It is inside out and not to be like the Pharisees and hypocrites that glitter on the outside and appear holy, but on the inside, they are full of greed and ask people to do the things that they cannot do.

"Woe to you, teachers of the law and Pharisees, you hypocrites! You clean the outside of the cup and dish, but inside they are full of greed and self-indulgence." (Matthew 23:25)

You will live to fulfil your calling, purpose, and destiny. The words of Apostle Paul will become your testimony and statement.

I have fought the good fight, I have finished the race, I have kept the faith. (2 Timothy 4:7)

You will defeat the last enemy as you overcome death and live into eternity, as the sting of death is sin. But we have been translated from the kingdom of darkness into His marvellous light, and instead of death, we shall put on incorruption, and this mortal must put on immortality. Thanks be to God, who has given us victory over death.

"52 in a flash, in the twinkling of an eye, at the last trumpet. For the trumpet will sound, the dead will be raised imperishable, and we will be changed. 53 For the perishable must clothe itself with the imperishable, and the mortal with immortality. 54 When the perishable has been clothed with the imperishable, and the mortal with immortality, then the saying that is written will come true: "Death has been swallowed up in victory." 55 "Where, O death, is your victory? Where, O death, is your sting?" 56 The sting of death is sin, and the power of sin is the law. 57 But thanks be to God! He

gives us the victory through our Lord Jesus Christ. (1 Corinthians 15:52-57)

You will receive the power to live a faithful life through the Spirit of God, who will help us to revere God. Unfaithfulness on the part of God's people is identified with adultery. Marriage is a metaphorical image of 's relationship with Israel. Adultery is a grievous sin—a sin against one's body—which the Israelites committed by worshipping other gods.

1 The word of the Lord came to me: 2'Son of man, there were two women, daughters of the same mother. 3They became prostitutes in Egypt, engaging in prostitution from their youth. In that land their breasts were fondled and their virgin bosoms caressed. 4The elder one was named Oholah, and her sister was Oholibah. They were mine and gave birth to sons and daughters. Oholah is Samaria, and Oholibah is Jerusalem.

5'Oholah engaged in prostitution while she was still mine; and she lusted after her lovers, the Assyrians – warriors 6clothed in blue, governors and commanders, all of them handsome young men, and mounted horsemen. 7She gave herself as a prostitute to all the elite of the Assyrians and defiled herself with all the idols of everyone she lusted after. 8She did not give up the prostitution she began in Egypt, when during her youth men slept with her, caressed her virgin bosom and poured out their lust on her.

9'Therefore I delivered her into the hands of her lovers, the Assyrians, for whom she lusted. 10They stripped her naked, took away her sons and daughters and killed her with the sword. She became a byword among women, and punishment was inflicted on her.

11'Her sister Oholibah saw this, yet in her lust and prostitution she was more depraved than her sister. 12She too lusted after the Assyrians – governors and commanders, warriors in full dress, mounted horsemen, all handsome young men. 13I saw that she too defiled herself; both of them went the same way.

14'But she carried her prostitution still further. She saw men portrayed on a wall, figures of Chaldeans portrayed in red, 15with belts round their waists and flowing turbans on their heads; all of them looked like Babylonian chariot officers, natives of Chaldea. 16As soon as she saw them, she lusted after them and sent messengers to them in Chaldea. 17Then the Babylonians came to her, to the bed of love, and in their lust they defiled her. After she had been defiled by them, she turned away from them in disgust. 18When she carried on her prostitution openly and exposed her naked body, I turned away from her in disgust, just as I had turned away from her sister. 19Yet she became more and more promiscuous as she recalled the days of her youth, when she was a prostitute in Egypt. 20There she lusted after her lovers, whose genitals were like those of donkeys and whose emission was like that of horses. 21So you longed for the lewdness of your youth, when in Egypt your bosom was caressed and your young breasts fondled.

22'Therefore, Oholibah, this is what the Sovereign Lord says: I will stir up your lovers against you, those you turned away from in disgust, and I will bring them against you from every side – 23the Babylonians and all the Chaldeans, the men of Pekod and Shoa and Koa, and all the Assyrians with them, handsome young men, all of them governors and commanders, chariot officers and men of high rank, all mounted on horses. 24They will come against you with weapons, chariots and wagons and with a throng of people; they will take up positions against you on every side with large and small shields and with helmets. I will turn you over to them for punishment, and they will punish you according to their standards. 25I will direct my jealous anger against you, and they will deal with you in fury. They will cut off your noses and your ears, and those of you who are left will fall by the sword. They will take away your sons and daughters, and those of you who are left will be consumed by fire. 26They will also strip you of your clothes and take your fine jewellery. 27So I will put a stop to the lewdness and prostitution you began in Egypt. You will not look on these things with longing or remember Egypt anymore.

28'For this is what the Sovereign Lord says: I am about to deliver you into the hands of those you hate, to those you turned away from in disgust. 29They will deal with you in hatred and take away everything you have worked for. They will leave you stark naked, and the shame of your prostitution will be exposed. Your lewdness and promiscuity 30have brought this on you, because you lusted after the nations and defiled yourself with their idols. 31You have gone the way of your sister; so I will put her cup into your hand.

32'This is what the Sovereign Lord says: 'You will drink your sister's cup, a cup large and deep; it will bring scorn and derision, for it holds so much.

33You will be filled with drunkenness and sorrow, the cup of ruin and desolation, the cup of your sister Samaria.

34You will drink it and drain it dry and chew on its pieces – and you will tear your breasts. I have spoken, declares the Sovereign Lord.

35'Therefore this is what the Sovereign Lord says: since you have forgotten me and turned your back on me, you must bear the consequences of your lewdness and prostitution.'

36The Lord said to me: 'Son of man, will you judge Oholah and Oholibah? Then confront them with their detestable practices, 37for they have committed adultery and blood is on their hands. They committed adultery with their idols; they even sacrificed their children, whom they bore to me, as food for them. 38They have also done this to me: at that same time they defiled my sanctuary and desecrated my Sabbaths. 39On the very day they sacrificed their children to their idols, they entered my sanctuary and desecrated it. That is what they did in my house.

40'They even sent messengers for men who came from far away, and when they arrived you bathed yourself for them, applied eye makeup and put on your jewellery. 41You sat on an elegant couch, with a table spread before it on which you had placed the incense and olive oil that belonged to me.

42'The noise of a carefree crowd was around her; drunkards were brought from the desert along with men from the rabble, and they put bracelets on the wrists of the woman and her sister and beautiful crowns on their heads. 43Then I said about the one worn out by adultery, "Now let them use her as a prostitute, for that is all she is." 44And they slept with her. As men sleep with a prostitute, so they slept with those lewd women, Oholah and Oholibah. 45But righteous judges will sentence them to the punishment of women who commit adultery and shed blood, because they are adulterous and blood is on their hands.

46'This is what the Sovereign Lord says: bring a mob against them and give them over to terror and plunder. 47The mob will stone them and cut them down with their swords; they will kill their sons and daughters and burn down their houses.

48'So I will put an end to lewdness in the land, that all women may take warning and not imitate you. 49You will suffer the penalty for your lewdness and bear the consequences of your sins of idolatry. Then you will know that I am the Sovereign Lord.' (Ezekiel 23:1-49)

And at the forgiveness of their sin, God gave them a new name: **Hephzibah**. The new name of the Israelites indicates an intimate relationship of God as a husband with His bride. (**My delight is in her – Hephzibah**). They shall no longer be called forsaken, as they cannot be plundered anymore. When you make your body the dwelling place of the Holy Spirit, you shall not be plundered or robbed by your enemies, and all the years that the cankerworm has stolen from you shall be restored to you. Your deliverance will be so thorough that your enemies will not (be able to lift up their hands to fight you anymore). have to lift up their hands to fight you anymore.

"No longer will they call you Deserted, or name your land Desolate. But you will be called Hephzibah, and your land Beulah; for the Lord will take delight in you, and your land will be married." (Isaiah 62:4)

YOU WILL LIVE A SUPERNATU- RAL AND VICTORIOUS LIFE

Living a supernatural life means living above what is natural; it cannot be explained by any natural law. As a child of God, this is the kind of life that God wants you to live — a life that successively takes you from weakness to strength, from powerlessness to powerful- ness, from defeat to victory, etc. It is the Holy Spirit that can give you this kind of life as you grow in His presence constantly.

As a Christian, you cannot function well without the Holy Spirit. The Holy Spirit brings the supernatural to us and brings us into the supernatural. The presence of the Holy Spirit in our lives opens the portal to the supernatural. You will enjoy the supernatural provision that God has made available through His word as His word becomes applicable to you, enabling you to address any situation you are fac- ing. Because you love God and seek Him earnestly, you shall be strong and do exploits as you seek Him in the secret place of your prayer. You will be able to connect the spiritual realm to the physical for a turnaround in your situation.

For the word of God is alive and active. Sharper than any dou- ble-edged sword, it penetrates even to dividing soul and spirit,

joints and marrow; it judges the thoughts and attitudes of the heart. (Hebrews 4:12)

This is what God said concerning His word, so there is no impossible situation that can withstand God's words in the mouth of a believer. The supernatural life will become your way of living.

'However, as it is written: "What no eye has seen, what no ear has heard, and what no human mind has conceived" — the things God has prepared for those who love him.' (1 Corinthians 2:9)

This is the unlimited power of God for His children. When God is with you, there is no way that you can fail or be put to shame. With the indwelling of the Holy Spirit, you can do all things. He did so much during His time on earth, and He promised you that you would do more than Him because He had gone to be with His Father. You cannot do this if the Spirit of God is not in you. To access the power to do more than you can think of, you need to make yourself the altar of God, a living sacrifice. Make your heart His dwelling place. It is then that the power of God can purify you so that the Holy Spirit can dwell in you, and you become His place of habitation.

We must not go about life in a physical and natural way without involving the Holy Spirit in a divine direction. You should take advantage of your duality with Christ. As a temple of God, you are a vessel of honour and a carrier of the Spirit of God. Once you recognise these facts and come to terms with them, you will realise that you are a spiritual being dwelling in a physical body that operates by the direction and leading of the Holy Spirit. You will give the Holy Spirit the wheel of your life and allow Him to take charge.

You will learn to take all things into prayer, dealing with them spiritually, and allowing God to take care of the physical manifestation of your needs.

Pray and continue to ask God to give you revelation at every stage of your life, leading you to the next level. Until you become a Christian who can see beyond the ordinary, you might not be able to attain a certain level of victory. It is very important. I pray for God's impartation upon your life, in Jesus' name. Amen.

We Will Be Fruitful and Not Be Barren

Fruitfulness is a divine instruction to the children of God. As a child of God, everything you do according to His will must prosper in your hands. Things should not die in your hands. Even when there is a casting down, there will be a lifting up for us in Jesus' name. Just as the Bible commands us to seek the kingdom of God and His righteousness, and every other thing shall be added unto us, so too shall fruitfulness be your inheritance. Even in drought, you will still be fruitful because you are like a tree planted by the river.

"That person is like a tree planted by streams of water, which yields its fruit in season and whose leaf does not wither — whatever they do prospers." (Psalms 1:3)

God will restore all your wasted years — the years that the cankerworm has eaten. You will no longer be plundered by your enemies. As you work, you will enjoy the fruit of your labour. Your yield will not go into the hands of taskmasters, as the Israelites were held in captivity for 430 years. Their tasks kept increasing under stringent conditions, and the sweat of their labour was enjoyed by Pharaoh and his taskmasters as they were made slaves.

21 They will build houses and dwell in them; they will plant vineyards and eat their fruit. 22 No longer will they build houses and others live in them, or plant and others eat. For as the days of a tree, so will be the days of my people; my chosen ones will long enjoy the work of their hands. 23 They will not labor in vain, nor will they bear children doomed to misfortune; for they will be a people blessed by the Lord, they and their descendants with them. 24 Before they call I will answer; while they are still speaking I will hear. (Isaiah 65:21-24)

Conclusion

Your body is a sacred dwelling place of God. It is the temple of God, and the reasonable service to offer is to present it as a living sacrifice — holy and pleasing to God. Your body is not merely flesh. Just as the temple in the Old Testament was dedicated as a place of worship and sacrifice, so too should our lives be consecrated for righteous living and holiness. The Holy of Holies was the inner chamber of the temple, and through the death of our Lord Jesus Christ — our Emmanuel, His incarnate name — God came to dwell with us, and we can experience Him in our hearts. Through the power that resurrected Jesus Christ from death, our once sinful bodies were rebuilt. We became vessels of honour, now housing the Holy Spirit, and as such, we cannot join our bodies with that of a harlot.

15 Do you not know that your bodies are members of Christ himself? Shall I then take the members of Christ and unite them with a prostitute? Never! 16 Do you not know that he who unites himself with a prostitute is one with her in body? For it is said, "The two will become one flesh." 17 But whoever is united with the Lord is one with him in spirit. 18 Flee from sexual immorality. All other sins a person commits are outside the body, but whoever

sins sexually, sins against their own body. 19 Do you not know that your bodies are temples of the Holy Spirit, who is in you, whom you have received from God? You are not your own; 20 you were bought at a price. Therefore honor God with your bodies. (1 Corinthians 6:15-20)

We are to take care of our bodies and treat them with dignity and respect. Just as Jesus Christ cleansed the temple by driving out merchants and money changers who had turned it into a place of commerce, so too must we do away with anything that does not glorify God in our lives so that His glory may be seen in us. As Jesus demonstrated this physically, we must keep our bodies holy and acceptable to God. As you encounter Christ, may you receive the power to live a holy life in Jesus' name. Amen.

www.ingramcontent.com/pod-product-compliance
Lightning Source LLC
Chambersburg PA
CBHW051320120626
46547CB00015B/2326